Linda Gray

Grow your own
Winter Food

How to harvest, store and use produce for the winter months

NH
NEW
HOLLAND

Published in 2011 by New Holland Publishers (UK) Ltd
London • Cape Town • Sydney • Auckland

www.newhollandpublishers.com

Garfield House, 86–88 Edgware Road, London W2 2EA,
United Kingdom

80 McKenzie Street, Cape Town 8001, South Africa

Unit 1, 66 Gibbes Street, Chatswood, NSW 2067, Australia

218 Lake Road, Northcote, Auckland, New Zealand

A catalogue record for this book is available from the
British Library

ISBN 978 1 84773 706 9

Publisher: Clare Sayer
Senior Editors: Amy Corstorphine, Marilyn Inglis
Designer: Geoff Borin
Production Controller: Laurence Poos

10 9 8 7 6 5 4 3 2 1

Reproduction by Modern Age Repro House Ltd, Hong Kong
Printed and bound in Malaysia by Times Offset (M) Sdn Bhd

Contents

Introduction

A couple of years into my adventure with an acre of land in rural France, I realized we were eating food from the garden right through the winter months as well as all the salads and fruits during the summer. On top of the financial benefits to be gained from growing our own food, the added bonus to this year-round production was the effect it had on our health.

What could be better than getting through a winter without one sniffle, cold or any other bug that circulates every time the temperature dips? So when you grow your own food, you are not only eating the best possible food on the planet, you are also getting plenty of fresh air and exercise, without having to go to the gym.

This book aims to help you through the sometimes overwhelming gardening experience with step-by-step instructions on how to grow your own food and the best ways to store it. There are also a few recipe ideas to help you make the very best of your crops.

Read through the gardening tips and helpful advice at the beginning of the book, especially if you've never attempted growing your own food before. But even for seasoned gardeners, there are always useful tips to pick up. At-a-glance tables provide a quick reference to sowing and harvesting times, pests and problems, and storing recommendations.

The second chapter has detailed instructions for growing a number of everyday root crops with traditional advice on how to store them. Some can even be left in the ground right through the winter months. In the third chapter are legumes and, although peas and beans are not generally grown during the winter months, they are exceptionally easy to grow and will store almost indefinitely, particularly if dried.

All the green vegetables listed in the fourth chapter grow happily through the colder months of the year, and some even improve in taste after being frozen on the plant a couple of times.

Herbs are a must-have if you want to get the most from your crops, and they are also very accommodating plants to grow, as you will see in the fifth chapter. Many can be grown indoors, in containers or outside in specially prepared herb beds. Herbs are also great companion plants to grow in your vegetable patch to deter pests and viruses from damaging your valuable fruit and vegetable crops.

And the last chapter focuses on fruits. Usually considered a summer-only crop, there are a surprising number of hybrid fruits available now that will crop right through the autumn and early winter. Those that don't will store well in a variety of different ways.

Not only is gardening a creative pastime, it also helps you exercise gently, breathe in the fresh air and just as importantly, gets you in touch with the earth. The soil contains natural antibiotics and a regular dose of nature combined with eating the best organic food on the planet will boost the immune system and help you stay healthy all year round.

Enjoy your gardening experience!

General gardening tips

If you are facing a mini-jungle behind your house or simply don't know where to start, the best way forward is in very small steps. It's easy to become daunted by the task in hand and one of the most common causes of back complaints — especially after the first sunny weekend of the year — is over-zealous digging and mowing.

Take it slowly. The garden is an on-going project and should never really be 'finished'. Plants grow, change shape, are replaced and need a certain amount of maintenance to keep them healthy. It is possible to buy an 'instant' garden these days, but it will never have the same appeal or produce the same kinds of crops as a traditional garden that has been lovingly created.

Enjoy your garden

Where do you start? The best way to get the most from your outdoor space is to make a plan. Putting your ideas and thoughts on paper will make the way forward a lot clearer and you can tackle one part of your plan at a time.

Spend a little time in the garden before you start. Looking out of the window won't give you a full picture no matter how wonderful your patio doors are. Get out there, even if it's for a few minutes every day, to observe and answer a few important questions:

- Where are the sunniest spots in the garden?
- What parts of the garden does the sun never reach?
- Is the soil well drained and are there any water-logged areas? Does the water sit in one spot?

Decide where your fruits and vegetables will grow. Pick the sunniest place if you can. Although some plants prefer a bit of shade during the day, most will benefit from a sunny spot.

Make sure the soil is well drained in this area as few plants will grow successfully in too much water. One exception to this rule is watercress.

Another thing to check is the pH balance of the soil. A pH-testing kit is readily available at most large garden centres or garden suppliers. It's useful to know whether your soil is heavy on the acid side, as different species of plant will thrive in different soil types. Brassicas (cabbage, broccoli, swedes) won't thrive and develop well in an acidic soil. If your soil is out of balance for what you want to grow, adjust it well before you start sowing seed or placing plants. Dig in some lime or other organic material specially for the

job, and let it settle. This is probably best done in early spring as soon as the soil is workable, or at the end of summer in preparation for spring plantings.

Think about all your garden needs. If you have children, a play area is probably a good idea unless they are all keen gardeners. Include pathways, however simple, to allow for movement, access and easy maintenance. And most importantly, create a space to relax. Whether it's a comfy chair on the patio or a purpose-built garden seat around the apple tree, you should always try to incorporate a seating area in your garden plan. A place to relax and to think about the next garden activity is an absolute must.

Ideas

There are many ways to get the most out of your garden space and it's easy to get carried away with the choices available. Try to keep to a modest plan if you are just beginning to garden and build up slowly. Even if you have to hand a whole area over to nature for a year or two, it is not the end of the world. In fact, a wild area of the garden will attract bees, butterflies and maybe even a few friendly frogs, which are always welcome garden guests. Amphibians will keep the slug population down, which in turn could save many of your young plants. Slugs and snails are the gardener's nightmare, since they can devour a whole line of newly germinated lettuces in a single sitting.

Bees will help pollinate the plants all round the garden, and of course butterflies are always welcome visitors too. Having said that, the cabbage white butterfly should be watched closely. Once the cabbage white lays her eggs on the underside of your cabbage leaves, the caterpillars that hatch after a few days can devour the whole plant in the same easy fashion as the slugs can with the lettuces.

So to get going in your garden, the first step is to not worry about getting it all done in one go. Introducing even one new plant every season or every year is progress whatever way you look at it. It's often said that you should live in a house for 12 months before you start making changes to it. The same could be said of the garden. It's good to know what you are dealing with before you start. And your garden should be an extension of your home, not an extra chore. When you make plans and allow yourself enough time to do it, a garden can become a relaxing, healthy and very inexpensive hobby.

Vegetables

There's nothing more rewarding than growing vegetables in your garden for family and friends to enjoy. Although there is an initial outlay and a certain amount of 'work' involved, when you pick fresh produce straight from your own vegetable patch, it always feels like free food.

Your vegetable patch should generally be in a bright airy spot sheltered from the wind, and preferably in a sunny position. Make sure you know where the sun stays the longest during the day.

You could dig over a large square to grow your vegetables or go for smaller beds. 'Potagers' were invented by the French to grow more crops in a smaller space without adding to the workload. Create

ABOVE *Wintery frosts cover the hedges and remaining crops within this 'potager'-style garden.*

small square beds and plan to grow vegetables in the middle and herbs around the edge if you want to imitate the 'potager' idea. However, this is your space and you should grow what you feel is best for your region, your garden area and your family.

Root crops need depth of soil, so if you have very shallow topsoil in your garden, you may have to create raised beds and ship in some topsoil. Alternatively, you could build it up yourself over a few years, using soil from your own compost heap.

Acquire some well-rotted manure if the soil seems to be tired and lacking in nutrients. When you get in touch with your garden, you will be able to tell

ABOVE *An apple tree, heavily laden with ripe fruit, is touched with a gilding of autumnal frost.*

instinctively if the soil is healthy and rich enough to feed your fruit and vegetable crops. If it seems a little on the poor side, dig in some well-rotted manure or compost to add nutrients to the soil before you start. Fresh manure should not be added to the soil just before planting as it will be too strong for very young plants. Dig it in at least a month or so before planting. Or spread manure at the beginning of the autumn.

When you are sure the soil is healthy and deep enough to accommodate your crops, the area should be dug over when it's not too wet. Don't try and dig over soil that is very wet and heavy. It not only hurts your back, it can also change the consistency of the soil, causing it to clump together and reduce its ability to release nutrients for your plants to take up.

Every crop you grow will draw nutrients from the soil, and the soil should be replenished as often as you feel necessary, but at least once every couple of years if you want to grow healthy crops. Make feeding the soil a regular habit, by spreading organic fertilizers over it or digging them into the soil as soon as you have cleared a space.

Plan to rotate your crops every year. Planting the same crops in the same place will encourage diseases and draw the same nutrients from the soil. Rotating crops helps prevent these problems and it's worth breaking your vegetable-growing areas up into three or four working spaces.

Plants in the same family should not be planted in the same spot year after year either. For example, potatoes, tomatoes and sweet peppers all belong to the same group of plants and can pass on unfriendly diseases though the soil.

Fruit

You don't need an orchard-sized garden to grow fruit these days. There are many miniature fruit trees available from good garden suppliers. Always make sure you check the manufacturer's growing instructions and recommendations before you buy so you know you have the right space for your plant. There's no point in putting a sun-loving peach tree in a shady place in your garden. You may be able to keep the tree alive but it's doubtful it will ever produce a good crop of fruit.

Native trees are always a good starting point if you want to grow fruit or other trees in your garden. These tend to be more resistant to local bugs and viruses and will cope with the weather conditions far easier than plants originating from other climates.

Larger-growing trees often need little or no maintenance and will carry on cropping year after year, although care must be taken when planting. Position your larger tree carefully, especially if it is likely to grow to a whopping 9 m (30 ft) high.

Some fruit trees can be trained to fan out over a fence or a wall. There should also be pruning instructions provided with the tree when you buy it. These fruit trees have generally been grafted onto a sturdy rootstock and can be resistant to many diseases.

As well as fruit trees, soft fruits, shrubs and perennial plants can also be incorporated in your garden. Strawberry beds are fairly easy to maintain and will go on year after year with a little care and attention, rewarding you with the best-tasting strawberries you have ever eaten. Likewise, raspberry and blackberry canes are worth planting for their luscious fruits that can be stored for winter eating.

Herbs

Planting a herb garden really is a wonderful way to brighten up your outdoor space. The good thing about herbs is that most will grow well in containers so can be planted in pots on the patio or balcony. Many can even be grown on a sunny windowsill. Herbs tend to crop most of the year round. Some are evergreen and others can be dried and stored for the winter months.

Plan your herb garden carefully and it will thrive for many years to come with very little maintenance required. Herbs can be strategically placed to give off the most delicious scents when brushed against and many have the added bonus of deterring bugs and pests from your vegetable crops. Growing a few in your vegetable patch will not only help to protect your plants, you will also remember to pick them.

Themes

A garden theme can take the whole garden space into a new sphere entirely. Colour co-ordinated flowers create a spectacular focal point to your garden, as will a herb garden or a rose bed.

Plants can be grown specifically to attract butterflies or bees. Make sure you have a small puddle of water available for wildlife to encourage return visits to your garden. Water features in a garden not only provide excellent feng shui and are beautiful to look at, they can also be a practical addition to the space. Watercress, for example, can be grown in running water. Frogs and toads will be attracted to your garden if you have a pond available for them.

Even if you don't have a large garden area, a patio can become a thing of beauty rather than just an extra surface to sweep from time to time. Grow herbs and flowering shrubs in attractive containers. Old pots can often be picked up at car boot sales or charity shops, and, with a little creative flair, can be turned into very appealing containers for your patio.

Make a plan

Once you have decided what you want from your garden space, draw up a plan. It does not necessarily have to be to scale, although you will get a better idea of what you need if you have taken the time to measure out the garden and added a little precision to your drawing.

From the plan, you can work out what materials, tools and equipment you need for each part of the garden. Again, especially with a large garden, don't try to take on too much all at once unless you have an army of willing helpers and an unlimited budget.

Decide what you will be working on in the coming year and plan accordingly. Start growing food crops as soon as you can. Even if you only have a very small area dug, producing your own food will encourage everyone in the family to join in with the preparations the following year.

Keep a garden journal, and note down when you sow seeds or put plants out. Later you can jot down how each crop fared and either repeat next year if you had a good crop, or resolve to make a change or two if the results were a little disappointing.

Tools and equipment

Garden tools and equipment need to be kept in a dry space and the best thing you could have in your garden is a shed. But before you buy or build a shed, consider what you will be storing in it. If your garage is large enough, garden machines can be stored there rather than in a shed.

Hand tools, small tools, pots and other paraphernalia will need to be stored in a shed. It will also help keep the garden tidy. Pots lying around are a reminder that something needs doing. Having a shed with a shelf specially designated for pots will encourage everyone to tidy up after themselves.

Another way to store small hand tools, gardening gloves and a trowel, is to position a mail box or birdhouse with a cover in the vegetable plot. This saves searching in the shed if you just want to pop out to potter around for five minutes.

Tools need to be put under cover to protect them from weathering. Metal implements rust very quickly if left out in the rain and damp. Well-looked-after tools encourage use and will last many years.

Greenhouses

A greenhouse is definitely an advantage if you are intending to start your plants from seed. And some plants can continue to grow on in a greenhouse. Choose a greenhouse according to your needs and budget. There are mini-greenhouses available from good garden centres and online, and these will give your seeds a good start while not taking up too much room in the garden. These smaller greenhouses can also be placed on a patio.

Cold frames

Like a greenhouse, cold frames are a distinct advantage in cooler climates, providing much-needed protection for tender plants. A cold frame can be put together with a few sheets of glass and a little carpentry expertise, or you can buy them from local garden suppliers. Cold frames can be positioned next to a greenhouse, or simply placed on the edge of a vegetable patch. Position them carefully to avoid accidents and harm to children and pets.

Cloches

A cloche is simply a mini-polytunnel. Make one by bending long lengths of plastic tubing or similar material into an arch and pushing each end firmly into the ground forming a tunnel shape. Make sure there are no rough edges. Cover with a clear plastic sheet and weigh the plastic down along each length with bricks or logs to prevent it flying away in the first gust of wind. Again, cloches of all shapes and sizes can be found at garden suppliers.

A portable cloche can be popped over young plants at night if a frost is expected and then removed the next morning – a bit like a mobile electric blanket for tender plants in early spring.

Tools

Depending on what you are about to tackle in the garden, you will need various tools. If lawn areas and hedges need regular cutting or trimming, consider the following:

- Lawn mower
- Edge cutter
- Hedge trimmer
- Pair of strong sharp shears.

Make sure you know how tools work before you buy them. Handle them in the shop and make sure they are comfortable for you.

A large area intended for vegetable or fruit crops may be easier to plough or rotivate. Look into local hire shops or make a deal with a local farmer.

Tackling a small area at a time will require hand tools, and they will eventually be needed all over the garden, so consider them carefully. Don't buy too cheaply. Weak-handled or badly joined tools can cause accidents. Not every tool in the garden centre has to be bought to begin gardening. Start off with the following as basics:

- Sharp-edged spade
- Garden fork
- Hoe
- Rake

Hold the tools in your hands before you buy them. A spade with a handle that is too short will cause unnecessary back strain as will anything that is too heavy. If you can hardly lift it when it's in the shop, you won't be able to use it in the garden very well. Buy sensibly for your own physique and strength.

Don't buy very cheap tools. They can bend, buckle and break easily and will have to be replaced. The extra investment in quality tools is worthwhile. In a larger

ABOVE *A bed of lettuce seedlings under a cloche. Use an old tablespoon to prick out seedlings when planting out.*

garden, you may want to buy tools with brightly coloured handles so you can spot them easily at the end of a gardening session. Or alternatively, paint them a bright colour yourself so that they stand out against the garden background.

Recycled tools
Old dessert or tablespoons are perfect for transplanting small plants. And an old table fork can be used to agitate the soil gently around plants in pots.

Other tools and equipment
There is so much garden paraphernalia available to buy and, because it's so much fun wandering around a garden centre, it's easy to fill the shed with stuff you really don't need and will probably never use.
- Be practical and buy what you need to start your garden, adding more tools and equipment as and when you need them.
- Buy a strong hand trowel that feels comfortable to use in your hand.

ABOVE *Planting in biodegradable pots allows you to plant on without disturbing the seedlings' delicate root structure.*

• A pair of good-quality sharp secateurs is a wise investment when pruning fruit bushes, roses or other small shrubs and plants.

• Strong gardening gloves are invaluable to protect your hands against stinging nettles, sharp thorns and staining of the skin. If you have any plant allergies, you must wear gloves. Try them on in the shop. Again, it's best to buy a good pair of gloves. There are 'bionic' styles of gardening gloves available although you may find they are not flexible enough for you.

• Garden shoes: However tempting it is to stroll outside in your slippers on a nice sunny day, they are not practical footwear for the garden. A good sturdy pair of boots should be worn to protect your feet when digging or using other sharp tools; they also give you some stability while using tools with which you may not be familiar.

If you are intending to sow seeds you will need seed trays and individual pots according to the needs of your particular seeds. Root crops are generally always sown directly outside, so if you are only planning to grow a few roots this year, you probably won't need seed trays or pots at all.

However, if you have trays and pots available you may just use these to try your hand at a few other crops. Most summer vegetables are started off in early spring in trays or pots and are kept warm and watered until transplanted into the garden later on.

Try to buy fairly sturdy pots and trays so you can use them more than once. The very flimsy ones are awkward to use and break easily.

Biodegradable pots are very useful to have. The whole pot is planted into the soil when the plant is ready to be put outside. This saves disturbing the plant and prevents damage to the roots. Root crops can fork or split when transplanted but this can be avoided if individual biodegradable pots are used. See the individual growing advice later on in the book to find which roots can be started off this way.

Free pots and seed trays

• Biodegradable pots can be made using a pot-making kit, available from good garden suppliers, or by simply rolling a couple of layers of newspaper around something like a rolling pin and then folding under the bottom edge to form a pot. Fit these closely in a seed tray before filling up with compost. They won't last long, but should just about make it until you need to plant them out in the garden.

- The cardboard tubes of kitchen paper or toilet rolls can also be used as biodegradable pots. Make a point of collecting these – cut the longer tubes in half and you have two for the price of one.
- Plastic yoghurt and dessert pots are fine for small plants. Make sure they are washed, rinsed and dried well, then punch a couple of drainage holes in the bottom of each one.
- Non-plastic or paper egg cartons and trays make ideal biodegradable pots for individual plants.
- Old paint trays are a good alternative to seed trays. Wash and rinse well. Dry thoroughly and punch some drainage holes in the bottom.
- Shallow wooden fruit and vegetable crates can be lined with card and also used as seed trays.

Free bits and pieces

- Keep old ice lolly sticks to use as pot markers. The wooden ones are easy to write on with a pen or pencil – no special marker pen required.
- Save used wooden skewers to mark row ends in the seed bed or garden.
- Clear plastic sheets are invaluable in the garden to protect young plants from cold nights and to give your seeds an extra boost in the greenhouse.
- Check packaging material before you throw any of it away – some of it might be handy in the garden.
- Old wire coat hangers that have been bent out of shape can be bent into a cloche shape and used as a frame for clear plastic to cover your smaller plants.
- Clear plastic mineral water bottles can be cut in half and used to protect individual plants on cold nights.
- Old CDs or silver foil strung across a fruit bush or bed will frighten the birds away from your crops.
- Use wire fruit and vegetable baskets as hanging baskets. Hang one outside the kitchen door with a few herbs growing in it.
- Recycle household items such as cutlery, pots and pans, cups, bowls and teapots to use in the garden. It doesn't matter if they only last a season if they are free.

Soil for free

You can also produce your own free organic compost by building a compost heap. There are composting tumblers available on the market and these are perfect if space is limited. Otherwise, build one yourself. Ideally, the compost heap should be accessible and easy to reach from the house so it's not a chore to take the vegetable peelings out.

Don't build the compost heap in a sunny spot. A shady part of the garden will be perfect. Make sure you have air flow for the heap to breathe and break down the organic matter. Wooden slats around the sides of four posts positioned in a square work well. The bottom slats of one side should be removable so you can dig out the fresh compost from the bottom of the heap when it's ready.

All vegetable peelings and grass clippings can be composted, although grass clippings are ideal to use as mulch around your plants. Spread clippings around lettuces and cabbages to keep the bottom leaves clean and the weeds away. Water the mulch after spreading to flatten. Don't mulch too high or too close around your plants or the stems may rot.

Pine needles and other hedge clippings may be used, but they tend to be more acid in content, so only mulch around the plants that like acid soil if you are using pine clippings.

Fresh compost can be spread over the vegetable plot in the autumn months to nourish the soil. Or dig into the ground a month or two before planting your crops.

NB: Always use fresh compost rather than garden soil for your pots or trays of seeds and seedlings. When planting out, mix the compost from the pots with the garden soil and plant your new plants in this mix.

Seasonal sowing and harvesting

Although we tend to associate sowing and harvesting with spring and autumn respectively, many crops can be sown and harvested at other times. The charts below show at a glance the sowing and harvesting times for all the crops in this book. Seasonal guides are given but it is always best to go by the weather, your knowledge of your own climate and your instincts. Also check the instructions given on your seed packets for regional variations.

Crop	Sowing/planting	Harvesting
Potatoes	Late summer (with plastic or glass cover towards end of year)	Late winter onwards
	Spring (main crop)	Summer–early autumn
	Midwinter (under cloche)	Spring
Carrots	Late winter–early spring (under cloche)	Summer
	Spring–summer	Summer–autumn
Swede	Late spring–early summer	Early autumn–early spring
Turnips	Early spring (summer varieties)	Midsummer
	Summer (main crop)	Early winter–midwinter
Beetroot	Spring–summer	Summer–autumn
Green Beans	Late spring–early summer (French Beans)	Summer–autumn
	Late spring–early summer (Runner beans)	Summer–early autumn
Broad Beans	Spring	Summer
	Late summer–early autumn	Early spring
Peas	Spring–summer	Summer–autumn

Crop	Sowing/planting	Harvesting
Kale	Late summer–autumn	Winter–early spring
Brussels Sprouts	Spring	Winter–early spring
Winter Lettuce	Late summer–autumn	Autumn–spring
Sage	Spring (seed)	From following spring
	Late summer–autumn (cuttings, layering)	From following summer All year round when established
Rosemary	Spring (indoor seed)	From following spring
	Early summer (outdoor seed)	From following summer
	Late summer–autumn (cuttings, layering)	From following summer–autumn. All year round when established
Thyme	Spring (indoor seed)	From following spring
	Early summer (outdoor seed)	From following summer
	Late summer–autumn (cuttings, layering)	From following summer–autumn. All year round when established
Garlic	Early spring	Summer–autumn
	Autumn	Spring
Chives	Early spring (seed)	From following autumn
	After flowering (root division)	When plants have settled and are growing again All year round when established
Parsley	Early spring (seed)	Summer–late autumn
Apples and Pears	Autumn–winter (one- or two-year-old trees)	Late summer–autumn
Strawberries	Early spring (seed)	Following summer
	Late summer–early autumn (plants)	Early summer, some varieties until late autumn
Blackberries	Late summer–autumn	Summer–autumn
Blackcurrants	Autumn–spring	Summer–autumn

Practical tips

There are so many variables in the garden, that the better armed you are against problems, the more successful your crops will be. The state of your soil, the weather and a vast collection of garden pests can conspire against even the most well-informed gardener.

These practical tips cover many of the common problems and will help you get the most out of your garden regardless of its size.

The soil and the weather

If you don't have well-drained soil, either incorporate sand or other organic material to increase the drainage or build raised beds. The roots of your plants will rot in waterlogged soil, in particular those plants that grow through the winter months. A touch of frost will freeze water in the soil very quickly and if the water doesn't get them, the frost will. So make sure your plants are in a well-drained spot.

No matter how conscientious a gardener you are, if bad weather strikes there is very little that can be done. However, most gardeners tend to get very good at predicting the weather over the years, and with a little practice and observation, everyone can do it. Ignore the weather forecast. Pop outside and smell the air, look at the clouds, feel the temperature. Then imagine how your plants are coping.

Rain

Of course we need rain, but if you have recently sown a delicate line of seeds, a sudden heavy shower could wash them away in seconds. A simple cloche popped over the seeds before it rains will protect them. Don't forget to remove it though. Constant high rainfall may wash nutrients through the soil too quickly for your crops to take them into their roots. Feed the soil fairly frequently if there has been more than average rainfall.

Don't assume the spring rains will be enough water for your newly planted trees. If there hasn't been a heavy rainfall every week or so, new trees in particular will need deep watering.

After a shower of rain, pop out into the garden if you can and pull the weeds. It's much easier to pull up the whole plant including the root when the ground is soft – easier on the back, too.

NB: When you need to water the garden, do it in the morning or evening – or both. Watering during the middle of the day can be harmful to your plants as well as wasting water that evaporates quickly in the sun.

Sun

Most crops benefit from a sunny spot in the garden, but not all. And although they may love the sun, plants are vulnerable to the sun's rays and can burn in hot midday heat. A little shade will prevent the soil from drying out too quickly as well as protecting plants from burning. Rig up a shade for your plants, but remember to remove it before night falls so that they can benefit from the early morning sun.

Wind

A cold strong wind can devastate tender crops. When planting, try to avoid windy areas in the garden, and always provide a support system for those plants that need it. If possible, position your shed in the windy spot to shield the garden from the worst excesses of the wind. Make sure, however, that the shed doesn't throw too much shade on your crops.

Snow and frost

Fruits and vegetables with high water content will almost dissolve before your eyes if caught in a heavy frost. However, there are a number of vegetables that will thrive quite happily through a frost and even

ABOVE *Sunlight and autumnal frost illuminate the beautiful structure of this Brussels sprout.*

under a blanket of snow will still be healthy and available to harvest. Some crops actually taste better for a touch of frost

Tender crops should be protected under glass or plastic if they are started early in the year. By mid to late spring it is usually safe to assume that all danger of frost has passed. But it's always a good idea to check on the seed packet for the manufacturer's growing recommendations for your region before you start to plant out or sow seeds.

Bugs and other problems

Some plants are vulnerable to all sorts of pests and viruses, although many winter crops are fairly robust. Whatever you are planting, slugs and snails can be a problem, so watch out for them. They can eat through the stem of every seedling very quickly, killing off all your young plants completely.

Crop	Problem	Treatment	Prevention
Potatoes	Blight	Bordeaux mix	Don't plant in soil where potatoes, peppers or tomatoes have grown in previous 2 years
Carrots	Carrot fly	No known organic treatment	Plant next to onions Cover with a purpose-made fleece
Swede	Club root	–	Plant in neutral soil rather than acidic
	Caterpillar	Remove by hand	Butterfly netting
Turnips	Club root	–	Plant in neutral soil rather than acidic
	Caterpillar	Remove by hand	Butterfly netting
Beetroot	Club root	–	Plant in neutral soil rather than acidic
	Caterpillar	Remove by hand	Butterfly netting
Green Beans	Black fly	Organic products available	Encourage ladybirds and grow marigolds nearby
Broad Beans	Black fly	Organic products available	Autumn-sown plants are usually safe from black fly. Encourage ladybirds, grow marigolds nearby
Peas	Mice	–	Coat seed in paraffin before sowing
	Caterpillar	Organic products available	Rotate crops (larva lives in soil). Cover with horticultural fleece from early summer

Crop	Problem	Treatment	Prevention
Kale	None known	–	–
Brussels Sprouts	Club root	Organic products available	Plant in neutral soil rather than acidic
	Aphids	Organic products available	Encourage ladybirds, grow marigolds nearby
Winter Lettuce	Root maggot	Organic products available	Water regularly and don't leave roots in the ground after harvesting
Sage	Waterlogging	None	Plant in well-drained soil
Rosemary	Not thriving	Add lime or other alkaline product	Plant in neutral soil
Thyme	Waterlogging	None	Plant in well-drained soil
Garlic	Bolting	Fold down leaves	Shade in very hot sunlight, water regularly
Chives	Onion fly	Organic products available	Don't plant near onions
Parsley	Not thriving	Feed soil	Plant in rich soil
Apples and Pears	Aphids, canker, mildew	Cut away canker from bark with sharp knife, treat with Bordeaux mix if necessary	Keep clean area around trees. Sweep up leaves, remove dead fruit etc.
Strawberries	Aphids	Organic products available	Encourage ladybirds, grow marigolds nearby
Blackberries	Aphids	Organic products available	Encourage ladybirds, grow marigolds nearby
	Rust	–	Keep area clean
Blackcurrants	Aphids	Organic products available	Encourage ladybirds, grow marigolds nearby
	Rust	–	Keep area clean

ABOVE *Slugs and snails are the gardener's enemy but there are a number of ecological ways of keeping them under control.*

Slugs and snails

There are organic slug repellents on the market and should be available at a good garden supplier or garden centre. Traditional slug deterrents can be useful as well:

- Break eggshells into fairly small pieces and spread around plants. Try not to leave any gaps – the slugs will find a way if they can.
- Sand around the base of your plants can help, although after a rainfall, it softens and the slugs don't take much notice. The drier and grittier the better.
- Slugs are attracted to beer. A small bowl of beer near your plants will distract them from dinner in favour of a pint. Don't rely on this method too heavily though.

Other pests

Other bugs and viruses can often be successfully treated and in some cases prevented entirely.

- Position herbs around the garden to deter bugs from your food crops. The strong scents repel many airborne nasties. Herbs tend to be fairly free from the threat of attacks but they are vulnerable to waterlogging, so plant in well-drained soil.

The good guys

Not all insects and wildlife are harmful to your garden, in fact, in some cases quite the reverse.

- Not only will they delight the children, frogs and toads will also keep the slug and snail population under control.
- Ladybirds eat bucketloads of aphids, protecting plants from black, green and white fly attacks.
- Bees are an absolutely essential part of successful gardening, helping to pollinate your plants. If you can, grow some flowering plants that bees love in order to encourage them to linger in your garden and pollinate your useful crops.
- Worms are a gardener's delight since they aerate and fertilize the soil.

There are a few other less conspicuous creatures that are well worth encouraging in your garden:

- Bats eat insects and can protect you from midges in the early evening.
- Praying mantis might not be such a well-known visitor to many suburban gardens, but if you see one, rest assured that it will be devouring harmful aphids as well as pesky mosquitoes.

Learning how to protect your own plants from the elements and from pests and diseases soon becomes second nature, especially after you have eaten your own home-grown crops and discovered just how delicious and nutritious they are.

ABOVE *Make friends with frogs – they will help you deal with slugs and snails and other pests.*

Alternative planting areas

The wonderful thing about plants is that they are not fussy where they live as long as they have the right amounts of light, warmth, nutrition and water. If a sufficient area of a garden or allotment is not available to you, there are other ways and means of producing your own food.

Containers

There are many plants that can be grown in containers, including some of the crops listed in this book:

Potatoes

These can be grown in deep containers, stacked rubber tyres or in purpose-built potato barrels. All of these containers can be kept on a patio or balcony. Try not to tuck the containers away too much as the potatoes will still need a reasonable supply of light and air to thrive.

Carrots

Trough-style containers work reasonably well for carrots. They must be deep enough to allow the carrots to develop fully.

Swedes, turnips and beetroot

These root vegetables could be tried in fairly large containers, although they tend to grow and develop more successfully in the vegetable plot.

Peas and beans

Some varieties will grow well in large containers but many need support systems so tend to be impractical for container growing. Large pots against a south-facing wall or fence, with a trellis or other support fixed to the fence or wall could work well.

Kale and Brussels sprouts

In theory kale and sprouts should do well in containers, but since they don't need protection from the cold, don't waste a valuable pot in a sunny spot.

Herbs

Almost all herbs can be grown in pots, although the larger types, such as rosemary and lavender are better in the ground as they grow and develop for years.

Apples and pears

Generally should be in the ground, although you may be able to find a hybrid that is small enough and grows well in your region in containers.

Strawberries

These grow very successfully in purpose-designed strawberry planters. They can be kept on a patio or in some cases, indoors in a conservatory.

Blackberries

Wild blackberries are not suitable container plants but some new hybrid types may work well for you in containers or large pots.

Blackcurrants

Smaller growing varieties may do well in containers, but they are generally happier in open ground.

Be adventurous when it comes to containers. A display of containers or large pots grouped together with herbs or salad crops tumbling from each can be a glorious focal point on a patio or in the garden.

Indoor growing

Unless you live in a particularly bright and airy house, many food crops won't get enough light to thrive except on a sunny windowsill. The best crops to grow indoors are herbs. A few pots of herbs on the kitchen windowsill will often last all year round and are less easy to forget about than those grown outside.

A conservatory is usually bright enough to grow fruit and vegetables. Containers of cherry tomatoes are attractive and useful, and you could try your hand at growing grapes or other fruits that benefit from a little extra protection.

Lemon trees in containers should have a space in the conservatory or a bright room in the house during the winter months, if you live in a cool climate.

Raised beds

For those who struggle with the physical bending involved in gardening, raised bed systems can be a huge advantage. The original concept of a raised bed was that you dig the ground over to about 1 m (3½ ft) across so that you can reach the middle from both sides. Then once the ground has been dug deeply and well-rotted compost incorporated, it's not walked on or dug again until the following year when you add more nutrients. This prevents the soil becoming compacted and more plants can be grown in a smaller space.

I have found that potatoes don't crop as well if you don't earth them up, but otherwise a raised bed system keeps the garden organized and is easy to maintain.

Another way of gardening in raised beds is to build

ABOVE *A raised bed system is a boon to gardeners who find it difficult to bend and reach – the whole bed is easily accessible.*

a trough shape from any materials that you have available and are sturdy enough, then fill with compost. Don't make a base on the trough or you will have trouble with drainage.

A more permanent raised bed should be built with brick or concrete blocks. Build two parallel walls about 30 cm (12 in) apart, and create ends to join the walls with bricks or use a sheet of aluminium or other material. Make sure the sides are solid so the soil doesn't move about.

Compost heaps sometimes reveal themselves as perfect 'raised beds'. When you see the odd courgette plant coming up on its own, encourage it to grow and use the courgettes.

Camouflage

Tall plants such as sunflowers or hollyhocks will cover an unattractive wall or fence, as well as an unsightly compost heap.

Or trail climbing crops over south-facing fences or walls. Plant close to the wall or fence and attach nails or other support system for the plants to cling on to. Soil close to a wall tends to dry out quickly so make sure your plants get enough water.

Storing methods

If you've had a good harvest, it's very likely you will need to store some of your crops. There are many ways of doing this, although some crops may store better using one method rather than another. The following methods are suitable for home-produced crops listed in this book.

NB: Never wash root crops before you store them. Dry in an airy or sunny spot for a few hours. Brush off excess soil. Always handle produce carefully to avoid bruising since damaged crops don't store well. Freezing produce made into soups, pies or other recipes is a good option for crops that don't freeze well in their natural state.

Crop	Storing options
Potatoes	• Vegetable clamp (see page 36) or in single layers in a cool dark place for several months • Purpose-built potato storage unit for several months • A few days in the vegetable rack
Carrots	• Vegetable clamp or in single layers in a cool dark place for several months • Barrel of sand for several months • A few days in the vegetable rack
Swede	• Best left in ground and used when needed until spring rainfall • Vegetable clamp or in single layers in a cool dark place for several months • A couple of weeks in the salad compartment of the fridge • A few days in the vegetable rack
Turnips	• Vegetable clamp for several months • Single layers in a dark airy place for a few weeks • Diced and frozen
Beetroot	• Pickled or bottled, will keep for many months • Vegetable clamp for several months • Salad compartment of the fridge for a week or two
Green Beans	• Frozen or bottled
Broad Beans	• Dried, frozen or bottled
Peas	• Dried, frozen or bottled

Crop	Storing options
Kale	• Best used straight from the ground all winter • A couple of days in the salad compartment of the fridge
Brussels Sprouts	• Best used straight from the ground all winter • Frozen • A few days in the salad compartment of the fridge
Winter Lettuce	• Best used straight from the ground all winter • A day or two in the salad compartment of the fridge
Sage	• Dried or frozen • Some varieties are evergreen so use throughout winter
Rosemary	• Evergreen so use throughout winter • Dried or frozen
Thyme	• Evergreen so use throughout winter • Dried or frozen
Garlic	• A week or so in the vegetable rack • Several months in plaits or laid out in boxes in a dark airy place
Chives	• Can be evergreen • A day or two in the fridge • Frozen
Parsley	• A few days in the fridge • Dried or frozen
Apples and Pears	• Wrap in newspaper or tissue, store in cardboard or wooden trays in single layers • Keep in a dry, airy place out of direct light • Dry in rings in a slow oven or home food dryer
Strawberries	• Frozen – although some taste and texture is lost • Jams and preserves
Blackberries	• Frozen – although some taste and texture is lost • Jams and preserves • Cordials, wine
Blackcurrants	• Frozen • Jams and preserves • Cordials

Root vegetables

Although most root crops are planted in the spring, they can be successfully stored for winter eating and keep very well. Swedes, for instance can be left in the ground well into late autumn. Your own organically produced vegetables will help keep the whole family fit and well during the winter months and root vegetables are especially nourishing and filling.

Generally all root crops need a good depth of soil that has not been fed with fresh manure in the previous month or so, since fresh manure will cause root crops to split or fork. If you think your soil needs feeding, dig in fertilizers a good month or two before planting or sowing seed in the spring. Alternatively, spread well-rotted manure over the ground during the previous autumn or winter so that the nutrients have ample time to be incorporated into the soil.

Potatoes

Strictly speaking, potatoes are tubers not roots, but for our purposes we will consider them as a root vegetable since they grow under the ground and are a nutritious and delicious family standby.

Although most folk will tell you not to grow potatoes because they are cheap to buy and hard work to grow, this is turning into a bit of a myth. For one thing, potatoes aren't particularly 'cheap' any more, and they can be grown in barrels, stacked rubber tyres or even a deep bucket if necessary, meaning far less physical work is involved.

Purpose-designed potato barrels can be bought from garden centres or other garden suppliers and these are useful in small gardens or for those with no garden at all. A potato barrel can stand on a patio or in a quiet corner of the garden, as long as it's a bright enough spot. You can leave the potatoes to just get on with the job of growing with very little input from you.

Seed

During the war years, in order to save money, cut-up pieces of potato were planted and often grew into healthy plants, producing many new organic potatoes. However, this method is a little hit and miss, as we tend to buy potatoes in plastic bags these days that have had a certain amount of processing along the way.

To get the most out of your potato harvest, start off with specially grown seed potatoes. Each one should be not much bigger than a golf ball and should look healthy and fresh.

There are a number of varieties of potato seed available at good garden suppliers. 'Desiree' and 'King Edward' are popular main crop choices. Try a late variety such as 'Maris Peer' – these need planting in late summer and should be ready to harvest and eat around midwinter.

Before you plant, lay the seed potatoes in single layers on a tray, in egg cartons or in a shallow box and leave in a dark place to 'chit' or sprout shoots.

Once your seeds have shoots they are ready for planting – don't put them out too early unless you are intending to grow early potatoes, in which case cover them with a cloche or plastic covering of some kind.

Planting out

If you have space in your vegetable patch, it's definitely worth growing a couple of rows of potatoes. Don't choose an area where tomatoes, peppers or potatoes have been grown in the previous couple of years since

these vegetables all belong to the same family and can spread diseases to each other through the soil.

You'll need a good depth of soil and the ground should be dug over well before planting. Remove any perennial weeds, large stones and non-organic debris from the soil, then dig a trench. Tools can be found for making trenches – either hand or mechanical tools are available, but they aren't absolutely necessary.

Use whatever feels comfortable for the job in hand; sometimes a simple spade will do the job well, but if your soil is a little crumbly it may be better to find another way. Dig your trench about 15–20 cm (6–8 in) deep, and if you are planting more than one row of potatoes, leave about 1 m (3½ ft) between rows.

One of my best potato crops ever was started on a bed of comfrey. If you have comfrey available, pick the leaves and lay in the bottom of the trench, sprinkle a little soil over the top and then lay your potato seed,

ABOVE *Stored in a cardboard egg carton, these half-dozen seed potatoes have produced chits or shoots.*

shoots up where possible, on top of that. Allow about 30 cm (12 in) between each potato. The comfrey leaves help to release nutrients from the soil into the roots of your potato plants. If you haven't any comfrey leaves, it's not the end of the world. Simply lay your potato seed along the bottom of each trench, again 30 cm (12 in) apart. Cover with the soil you dug out and water the ground well.

Keep weed free and water regularly if the weather is dry. After a few weeks you will notice small bushy leaves emerging along the line. Try to wait until all the plants are up and showing if you can (there may be a 'dud' so don't leave it too long). The plants should be 'earthed up' at this point. Using a heavy rake or any other tool that works for you, pull the soil from both sides of the line and cover the newly emerging plants completely. Leave the soil loose on top of the mound and the plants. You will now have shallow trenches on either side of a long mound.

Make sure the ground doesn't dry out and remove the weeds as they emerge. A few weeks later, once the potato plants have poked through again, the whole earthing-up process needs to be repeated and then repeated again a few weeks after that.

Once the plants have been earthed up three times in total, you will have deep trenches on either side of a fairly large mound. Let the plants grow on from this point. The earthing-up process gives the roots a chance to expand and you will get far more potatoes using this method. Potatoes can also be grown in a raised bed system, although they tend not to crop as well if they aren't earthed up.

Care and maintenance

If the weather is particularly warm and muggy, your potato plants may be susceptible to the blight virus. Many growers spray their potato crops every few weeks during the growing season to prevent blight attacks. Use a Bordeaux mixture (copper sulphate and hydrated lime dissolved in water) or other organic product.

When the plants have flowered or are just starting to flower, treat yourself to a few tiny new potatoes. Scrape the earth away from the side of the mound next to a healthy plant and search for a few baby potatoes. Push the earth back once you've taken one or two potatoes from a plant. Don't take more than one or two potatoes from each plant. The potatoes left behind will carry on growing and developing as long as you re-cover them properly with the soil.

RIGHT *Seed potatoes are planted about 30 cm (12 in) apart in their trench with chits pointing up. Cover, then water well.*

Harvesting

When your potato plants have died back completely, the potatoes underground will have more or less finished growing. In the morning of a dry day, carefully fork around your plants, allowing a good area all round as the potatoes spread out; if you are very careful, you may not spear too many. It's almost impossible not to catch one or two with your fork. Don't try to store these ones, simply use them first. Cut away the rough-looking parts and have the rest for dinner.

Once you have dug round the plant, gently lift the soil and you'll be able to find the potatoes. The best way to do this is with your hands. Wear gloves to

ABOVE *Small potato plants emerging from the soil and are ready to be earthed up – raking soil over the entire plant.*

protect your skin if you need to. Push away all the earth and make sure you remove all the potatoes from the ground. Repeat the digging and lifting process with all your plants, then spread the potatoes over the dry earth for a couple of hours in the sun, turning as they dry. Don't leave them out overnight. When the skins are dry your potatoes can be stored.

Storing

Years ago (and to this day on some smallholdings), root vegetables were kept in specially prepared earth clamps for the winter. There's no reason why you shouldn't have a go at using this method of storage, especially if the winter isn't expected to be too wet.

Smooth out an area of ground where you have just dug out your potatoes or other root vegetables and firm down the soil with your feet. Dig a shallow trench around a circular area to deter hungry animals. Lay a 20 cm (8 in) depth of dry straw on the firmed-down circular area and pile your vegetables in the middle of the straw to form a cone or pyramid shape. Make sure the vegetables are completely dry before you do this.

Cover your vegetables with straw, then cover the whole thing with earth, leaving a ventilation hole at the top about 10–15 cm (4–6 in) across. Stuff this hole with straw. In a properly built clamp your vegetables will keep for a few months.

Potatoes can be stored successfully for many months as long as they are kept out of direct light and are not too damp or cold. Potatoes, like many vegetables, have a high water content and will rot if left to get wet or frozen. Either build a vegetable clamp as above or store your potatoes in single layers in stackable boxes. Always make sure the skins have dried thoroughly before laying in the box and never store in direct light or damp conditions. Potato storage units can be found in garden centres or other garden suppliers.

Vitamins

Potatoes are a valuable source of vitamin C and some B vitamins. They are also a good source of carbohydrates. In the past potatoes have been considered an aid to digestive problems and also dry skin and sores. They have only a trace of fat in their natural state. Potatoes with their skins are considered to be more nutritious than potatoes without, but however you prepare them, the honest spud makes a valuable contribution to the family diet.

Recipe ideas

Potatoes are probably one of the most versatile vegetables you can grow. Many dishes can be made and frozen for the winter months ahead, when the potatoes in your storage boxes or clamps are starting to get a bit too soft to use.

A fresh potato straight from your garden tastes like no other potato. Steam or lightly boil and serve as they are or with a sprig of mint to complement any roast dinner. If they have just been dug up, the skins will probably just rub off. Try not to peel your home-grown potatoes unless you haven't grown them organically of course.

Baked potatoes

One of the most popular ways to serve a medium to large potato is baked. Simply wash the potatoes before baking in a medium oven for an hour or until they are cooked right through. Serve with one of the following, or with any favourite filling:
- Plenty of butter, salt and black pepper
- Grated Cheddar with coleslaw
- Baked beans
- Tuna and sweetcorn with mayonnaise

Alternatively, split them, scoop out the flesh and mash with cheese and butter before spooning back into the skins. Grill for five minutes to brown them. Scoop out the flesh very carefully so you don't damage the skin too much.

Potato Dauphinoise

Creamy dauphinoise is particularly delicious served with a fillet steak and a crisp green salad, but is also a fantastic alternative way of serving potatoes as an accompaniment to a variety of dishes.
- Preheat your oven to 190°C (375°F/gas mark 5). Grease a large shallow baking dish with butter.
- Slice 1 kg (2 lb 3 oz) potatoes as thinly as you can, using a vegetable peeler or a very sharp knife. Layer evenly in the buttered baking dish, along with a finely sliced onion, seasoning as you go. Pour over 284 ml (10 fl oz) double cream and 75 ml (2½ fl oz) milk, dot over a little butter and cover the dish with foil.
- Place on a baking sheet and bake for 1 hour. Discard the foil and bake for a further 15–20 minutes, or until the potatoes are cooked through and golden.

Potato and chickpea curry

Potatoes work well in curries and this easy recipe takes just 25 minutes to whip together. The dish is packed with protein, so is really nutritious for vegetarians. If you prefer a less spicy curry, simply add less curry paste and go easy on the coriander.
- Cook 2 roughly chopped medium-sized potatoes in salted boiling water for 10–15 minutes until tender.
- Heat a little olive oil in a frying pan, add a finely sliced onion and cook for 5 minutes until soft. Stir in 1–2 tbsp curry paste, 300 g (10 oz) can of drained chickpeas and 250 ml (8 fl oz) cold water. Simmer for 5 minutes.
- Drain the potatoes, add to the frying pan along with a small bunch of chopped fresh coriander and stir over a low heat for a few minutes. Serve with steamed rice or naan bread.

Other ideas

- Spread mashed potato over cottage or shepherd's pie, sprinkle with cheese and brown under the grill. Or leave mashed potato to cool and roll into little balls to make croquettes. Coat in flour and fry in hot oil or bake in a moderate oven for 10–20 minutes.
- For a treat, make homemade crisps and chips. For chips, cut washed potatoes into chunky chips. Fry in hot oil until golden brown. For crisps, use a potato peeler or mandolin to slice potatoes very thinly and fry in hot oil for a couple of minutes.
- Boil, steam or roast or add to stews, soups and quiches for extra bulk and flavour. Make hash browns with left-over mashed potatoes.

Carrots

Carrots have been cultivated for thousands of years and many different colours of carrot were grown in kitchen gardens – even purple carrots had a place on the dinner table. In the 16th century, Dutch growers crossed a yellow and a red variety and produced the bright orange carrot we know and love today. It is possible to buy specialist seed for heirloom varieties, although the everyday seeds seem to do the job perfectly well if you are intending to grow a basic crop of orange carrots. If you have the space, time and inclination though, try a different coloured variety too.

Seed

It's always a good idea to buy your seeds from a reputable supplier. Cheap seeds can be old or damaged, and it will be a struggle to get any decent crops from them. Carrots are a root vegetable and require a certain depth of soil to fully develop. However, there are shorter, fatter varieties available that will grow well in only a few centimetres or inches of decent top soil. Read through the manufacturer's growing recommendations on the seed packet, preferably before you buy seeds, but definitely before you sow.

If you like the idea of growing different coloured carrots, you may have to go a little further afield to find a suitable variety, but it's worth the extra effort. Again, check on the depth of soil required for the carrots to fully develop.

Always sow your carrot seed *in situ*. Carrots, like most root vegetables, don't transplant well. It is possible to transplant, but the carrots will very likely 'fork' or split and twist into uncomfortable shapes.

Sowing

If your ground is tired or lacking in nutrients after being over-worked in recent years, dig in some organic compost or well-rotted manure a month or two before a spring sowing. Don't add fresh manure to your soil just before or after sowing carrot seed as this will, like transplanting, make them fork or split.

When you are happy with the soil, dig over as soon as it is workable in the spring. Remove any perennial weeds, large stones and non-organic debris. Large stones or lumps of concrete in the ground will inhibit the growth of your root crops. Fork after digging to break up the soil then rake over to a fine consistency.

As soon as the weather warms up, carrot seed can be sown. Check on the recommended sowing times for your particular variety. Some carrot seed should be sown earlier than others.

Sow very short lines of seed, up to 1 m (3½ ft) long, and rake the soil carefully over the top. Water gently and keep watering from time to time if there isn't at

least one shower of rain every day. The seeds won't germinate if left to dry out. They also won't germinate in waterlogged soil, so make sure the soil is well drained and don't over-water.

It's best to sow very short lines of carrot seed because once the seedlings are a couple of centimetres high, they will need to be thinned out. This is a laborious job if you have sown long lines of seed. If you can, thin out your seedlings when it is raining to deter the carrot fly that can damage your crops. The carrot scent is less pungent to the carrot fly when it is raining. Otherwise, water the ground first, then carefully remove weaker seedlings allowing a couple of centimetres between the plants you leave. Firm the soil gently around the remaining plants with your fingers. Water if necessary and leave to grow on for a few more weeks, then repeat the process. On the second thinning session, you should be pulling up very tiny carrots. These are edible and delicious, so throw them in the salad bowl rather than on the compost heap.

Care and maintenance

Thinning should be carried out at least once or twice per line to allow space for the roots to develop. Sow short lines of seed every couple of weeks so you have a constant supply, but not so many that the maintenance becomes too overwhelming. It may seem a lot of work to produce a few carrots, but the process isn't hard and it gives you a good excuse to pop out to the garden for ten minutes every now and then. And of course home-grown carrots are superb!

Seeds can take some time to germinate – anything up to six weeks is possible. Make sure your plants are watered and kept weed-free during the growing season. Carrots don't like to dry out, but apart from that they are fairly hardy plants. A little gentle surface hoeing every now and then will help aerate the soil and remove any weeds.

Don't feel you have to wait until each plant has fully developed before you pull them to eat. Always try to lift carrots from the row when the soil is damp to avoid tugging at the others too much. Loosen the soil gently around the plants with a fork if necessary.

BELOW *Carrot varieties don't just come in orange; they can vary enormously in colour, shape and size.*

Harvesting

Pull your carrots as you need them right through the growing season. They should all be harvested before the heavy autumn rains, and definitely before a ground frost, unless you have found a particularly hardy variety. Check on your seed packet for growing, harvesting and storage advice.

Loosen the soil around your carrots before pulling them from the ground. If they feel too firm to pull up, dig a little deeper before trying again. If you force the root, it may break. Leave the carrots to dry in the sun for an hour or two before bringing in to store.

Storing

Carrots can be stored in a vegetable clamp or spread out in trays and kept in a cool dark place for several months. Hanging them in sacks can also work well. Carrots can also be stored in barrels of sand, but that isn't always a viable option in a modern household these days. If you do go for the barrel method, watch out for mice invasions.

Never wash carrots before storing; they will rot very quickly. Simply dry in the sun or a dry place, then brush off any excess soil before storing.

Carrots can be frozen, although they do lose some of their texture and taste. Freeze in slices very quickly and remember to label before storing. Bottling is another option if you are set up to do so. Always store bottled vegetables out of direct light.

Vitamins

During the Second World War, pilots were given carrots in the belief that it would make them more able to spot their targets; it became a well-known saying that you should eat your carrots if you want to see in

ABOVE *Rows of young carrot plants that have been thinned once or twice and may need thinning again.*

the dark. Although this seems like an old wives' tale, there is some evidence to support the fact that carrots really do help your eyesight.

Carrots contain vitamins A, B1 and B6 and significant quantities of calcium and iron. Vitamin A is essential for good vision and one medium-sized carrot can provide all of your recommended daily intake of this vital vitamin.

Gardener's tip
Plant carrots and onions in lines next to each other. You will find that the scent from the onions deters the carrot fly and that from the carrots deters the onion fly.

Recipe ideas

Carrots are one of the foods that can be eaten in sweet or savoury dishes, and either cooked or raw. Carrot sticks make a great snack as you really need to chew them well, which tends to satisfy the snacking reflex quite nicely. They can also be peeled into thin ribbons or grated and served as a separate vegetable, as a garnish for a salad or any hot dish. Carrot cake is one of the most popular tea-time treats.

Quick and easy coleslaw

Mix grated carrots with grated white cabbage and finely chopped or grated onion, then stir in a half-mayonnaise/half-natural yoghurt dressing or any other combination you prefer. Crème fraîche or natural fromage frais can also be used. You might try adding a few broken walnuts, pine nuts or sunflower seeds for added crunch. Chill for 20–30 minutes before serving.

Garlic carrots

Scrub carrots well and rinse under running water. Peel carrots that you have bought or that have been grown non-organically. Slice into coins or cut into matchsticks and steam or boil for about ten minutes until tender. Remove from the heat and drain well. Return to the pan and stir in a crushed garlic clove, a tablespoon chopped parsley and a knob of butter. Put the lid back on the pan, give the pan a shake and leave for a minute for the carrots to absorb the garlic flavour. Serve hot.

Herby carrots

Prepare in the same way as garlic carrots but instead of adding garlic, add a tablespoon or two of your favourite chopped fresh herbs, depending on what you are serving them with. For example, stir in chopped fennel or dill leaves into the carrots to complement a fish dish. Or use mint if you are serving carrots with roast lamb. Coriander also works well with carrots and will add colour and flavour to an everyday meal.

Carrot and coriander soup

Soups are a great way to feed the family during the cold winter months and carrot soup is no exception. There are many recipes for carrot soup, but this one is simple to make and will appeal to all tastes. Go sparingly with the coriander unless you like your food on the spicy side.

● In a large pan, warm a little oil or butter and add to it 2 finely chopped onions and 6 prepared and sliced carrots. Stir and cook gently for 5–10 minutes until the vegetables are soft. Stir frequently to prevent them from burning. Add about 1 litre (2 pints) of vegetable stock, season with salt and pepper and cover the pan with a lid. Bring to the boil and then reduce the heat and simmer for about 20–30 minutes.

● Stir in a handful of chopped fresh coriander and bring back to the boil. Reduce heat again and simmer for another 10–20 minutes until thoroughly cooked. Check the seasoning and add a little more coriander or pepper if required.

● Remove from the heat and cool slightly then blend in a food processor or blender until smooth. Return to the pan and heat through very gently. Serve hot in individual bowls with a swirl of single cream or crème fraîche on top. Garnish with a sprig of fresh coriander.

● If you haven't got a blender or food processor, drain the vegetables, retaining the liquid then mash the vegetables with a potato masher. Stir the carrot mash together with the reserved liquid to form a smooth, creamy soup and then reheat as above. Soup (minus the cream) can be frozen in containers and kept for several months in the freezer.

Other ideas

● Add carrots to stews and casseroles to add bulk and flavour and plenty of nutrition.
● Cut carrots into strips and stir fry with green peppers and bean sprouts.
● Finely dice carrots and add to recipes for bolognaise and lasagne dishes.

Swede

Swede is delicious and has been neglected a little during the instant meal revolution. It is a hardy vegetable and will stay in the ground right through the winter with a little care. A close relative of turnip, swede is classed as a root vegetable, and is also a member of the brassica family. It tends to grow larger than turnip and usually has a purple-coloured area at the base. There are a few different varieties of swede available.

Also known as rutabaga, swede doesn't have as long a written record as other root vegetables but by the 18th century it had become an important garden crop in many parts of Europe.

Swede will benefit from a well-nourished soil. Dig in plenty of organic well-rotted compost or manure during the month or two before you sow the seed. Never put fresh manure or compost on the area before or after sowing as this will cause root crops to split and they won't develop well. Compost or well-rotted manure can also be spread over the ground in the previous autumn. Swede is generally sown in late spring and early summer so the ground should have plenty of time to settle.

Seed

There are a few different varieties of seed available from good garden suppliers. If possible, buy a variety resistant to club root, a disease that can affect all brassica plants and will destroy the roots.

Because swede is a brassica it doesn't like an acid soil and the pH balance should be about neutral. Acidic soil will contribute towards the possibility of club root as well, so make sure your soil is well balanced before you start growing this root vegetable.

Seed should be sown *in situ* as with all root crops, but can be successfully grown using biodegradable modules, where you plant out the whole pot to avoid any contact or damage to the roots.

Sow seed from late spring onwards. Check the manufacturer's growing recommendations on your seed packet, as varieties and regional needs may differ.

Sowing

Dig over your plot and remove any large stones, perennial weeds and non-organic debris, then rake over to a fine consistency. The area should be well drained and in a fairly sunny spot. If you have trouble getting your ground well drained, form a ridge with the soil and sow your seed on top of the ridge. The water then drains away from the plants and reduces the possibility of waterlogging.

Sow seed thinly along a line and leave about 60 cm (24 in) between lines. Remember you will need to allow around 25 cm (10 in) per plant eventually, so ensure you prepare fairly long lines if possible, and sow seed very thinly. When you choose the spot in your garden for swedes remember they can stay in the ground for much of the winter so plan accordingly.

Swede seed tends to germinate within a couple of weeks. When the seedlings are a few centimetres high they will need thinning. Make sure the soil is damp before you do this to avoid pulling out plants you want to leave in. Work along the row, removing weaker plants and leaving 25 cm (10 in) between each one to give them space to develop. (Double-check on any variations on your seed packet.) Don't attempt to replant the seedlings you pull out. Although it seems a waste, they won't grow well if you replant them.

Care and maintenance

When your plants are small, they should be protected from slugs and snails and flea beetle. The flea beetle arrives early in the year, so if you can hold off sowing your seeds until late spring, you may get away with missing them. Slugs and snails, however, are always around so do what you can to stop them attacking your young crops.

The other problem you may have with wildlife is the cabbage white butterfly. It lays its eggs on the underside of the leaves of brassica plants and within days the caterpillars hatch and devour everything in their path – usually your valuable crops. Keep an eye open for the beautiful but very crop-damaging cabbage white butterfly. Check on the underside of the leaves of your plants every day for eggs. If you find them, either scrape them off or remove the whole leaf and then compost it.

Keep the ground watered during dry periods and remove any weeds as they appear. If you are using

ABOVE *Prepare a ridge with the back of a rake along a line in order to sow swede seeds – sow thinly and thin out the seedlings.*

FAR LEFT *In the foreground a crop of swedes growing in a raised bed. Note the protective netting in the background.*

biodegradable pots, sow a few seeds in each pot and keep the soil damp but not waterlogged. When the seedlings are a few centimetres high, carefully remove the weaker ones, leaving one strong plant per pot. Then plant out the whole pot, leaving 25 cm (10 in) between each plant and grow on.

Harvesting

Swede can be stored for a couple of weeks after pulling, but they are so hardy and tolerant of frost and cold that they can be left in the ground right through the winter. Double-check on your variety just in case you have a frost-tender type. Fork around the whole plant carefully before attempting to pull up the root.

Swedes can be used as soon as they are about the size of a grapefruit, however, after the first frost they will be sweeter and more enjoyable. Take advantage of their resistance to the cold and leave your swedes in the ground until you need them.

Storing

Although this is one of the vegetables you can leave in the garden through the winter months, or until the rain gets too heavy in early spring, swedes will keep for several weeks after harvesting if required.

Dig up and leave to dry outside for an hour or two. Rub off any excess soil and store in a dry dark place until needed. Try to use within a week or two. Some swede varieties may store better than others so check the manufacturer's recommendations on your seed packet for length of storage options. Otherwise, if you have to dig them up, keep for only a week or two before using. They can also be stored in the salad compartment of the fridge for a couple of weeks.

Vitamins

As with all root vegetables, Swedes are rich in minerals including calcium, magnesium, manganese and potassium. Swede has a very low level of fat and also boasts vitamins A and C in its composition. Root vegetables are nourishing in the winter months and should be eaten regularly; they are also a good source of dietary fibre.

Swedes have a high natural sugar content especially after the first frost of the year. Enjoy your first swede after the first frost in a heart-warming stew or sustaining casserole.

Recipe ideas

Traditionally, swede has always been boiled and mashed and can be served with almost any main course. Its sweet flavour will complement any meal, including your favourite Sunday roast, and it is especially good with a gammon joint. Swede can also be eaten raw – grate it very finely and mix it into a winter salad for extra vitamins and crunch.

Herby swede mash

Peel and cut your swede into chunks. Put into a pan, cover with water and bring to the boil. Reduce the heat and simmer for 20 minutes or until the swede is tender and cooked right through. You could steam instead of boiling if you prefer. Once cooked, drain well and return to the pan. Mash using a potato masher or a fork, add a knob or two of butter, black pepper to taste and a handful of finely chopped fresh herbs of your choice. Mash again to mix well and serve hot.

Swede and bacon

Swede and bacon were made for each other and this is a great way to use up any uneaten swede.
● Peel and cut your uncooked swede into small cubes. Cook about 6 rashers of bacon (trimmed of fat and rind) in a little olive oil and remove the bacon. Drain on kitchen paper to remove excess oil.
● Peel and finely chop an onion and add it to the oil in the pan. Cook over a gentle heat until the onion is soft and translucent.
● Add the swede cubes and stir well. Cook over a low heat, stirring all the time until the swede is tender, then cut the bacon into pieces and add to the pan with a handful of chopped fresh parsley. Continue stirring and cooking gently until hot right through and serve with mashed potatoes.
● Leftover gammon can be used instead of bacon rashers. When reheating meat, make sure it's piping hot right through before serving.

Cornish pasties

Created originally for Cornish tin miners who, unable to return to the surface at lunchtime, would have this hearty pastry stuffed with meat and swede. This classic is just as popular today and there are endless variations for fillings, but the traditional version uses beef, potato and, of course, your delicious home-grown swede.

● To make 4 pasties, first preheat the oven to 220°C (425°F/gas mark 7). In a bowl, mix together the filling ingredients: 350 g (12 oz) rump or braising steak, finely sliced, 1 large onion, finely chopped, 2 medium potatoes, finely sliced and 1 medium swede, finely diced, and season with salt and pepper.
● Using 375 g (13 oz) ready-made shortcrust pastry, divide into 4 rounds and roll out to about 23 cm (9 in) across using a dinner plate to trim to shape. Firmly pack a quarter of the filling along the centre of each round, leaving a margin at each end. Brush the pastry around the edge with beaten egg, carefully draw up both sides to meet at the top, then pinch the edges together to seal.
● Carefully lift onto a baking tray, brush with the remaining beaten egg and put in the preheated oven. After 10 minutes in the oven, turn the temperature down to 180°C (350°F/gas mark 4) and cook for a further 45 minutes until golden. Cornish pasties are perfect for lunchboxes, picnics or as a main meal with green vegetables.

Neeps and tatties

'Neeps' are what the Scots call swedes, and this is the traditional accompaniment to haggis. Neeps are a dish that is best made the day before you want to serve it.
● Preheat the oven to 200°C (400°F/gas mark 7). Cut 4 large potatoes into chunks and cook in a pan of boiling salted water for 5 minutes. Drain the potatoes, return to the pan and put back on the heat for a couple of minutes to dry out.

● Pour 3 tbsp olive oil into a large roasting tin and heat in the oven until hot but not smoking. Stir the potatoes into the hot oil and put in the oven for 50 minutes, turning occasionally. Meanwhile, roughly chop a medium swede and cook in boiling salted water for 50 minutes until soft and tender.
● Drain the swede and add to the roasted potatoes. Mash together, keeping everything quite chunky and leave to cool. When ready to eat, dot with a little butter and return to the oven for 25–30 minutes.

Other ideas
● Swede is a perfect vegetable to add to stews and casseroles. Add swede early on in the cooking time as it generally takes longer to cook than carrots or potatoes.
● The leaves of the swede plant can be eaten as well as the root. Don't strip one plant completely, otherwise the root won't develop, but you can steal a few leaves here and there from time to time. Steam or boil as you would spinach and serve hot as a side vegetable.

Turnips

A traditional winter crop, turnips have been cultivated for thousands of years and were even used as currency in trading. This root vegetable was very common before the potato became more popular and turnips took second place. Turnips are an excellent crop to grow later in the year, but won't grow well in long hot summers; in fact they tolerate the first cold nights of autumn and even winter very well.

Turnips are best eaten when fairly small although they are good even when they have reached a more substantial size and, like swedes, are wonderful in sustaining winter dishes.

Seed

Turnips can be grown for their greens as well as the roots, but care should be taken not to pick too many leaves off each plant. Different varieties can be grown specifically for the root or for the greens. Choose your seeds carefully, according to your own needs.

As with other root crops, turnip seed should be sown *in situ* in well-prepared ground. It is possible to sow turnips in individual pots as long as they are biodegradable. You can plant the whole pot out later to avoid any damage to the roots or having to remove the seedling from the soil.

If you are using this method, when the seedlings are a few centimetres high, wet the soil in the biodegradable pots and then very carefully remove the weaker seedlings. Leave behind one strong plant per pot to grow on. It is, however, preferable to sow your turnip seed directly into the ground where you plan to grow your crop. Check your packet for specific instructions pertaining to your variety.

Sowing

Prepare your ground well. Choose a sunny well-drained spot in the garden and dig over to a good depth to give your root crops a chance to develop properly. Remove any perennial weeds, large stones and any non-organic debris.

Don't dig in any manure or compost unless it is well-rotted, and ideally this should be incorporated into the soil at least a month or two before you plan to sow the seeds.

Rake over the soil to a fine consistency, make a shallow drill and sow your seeds thinly along the row. Leave about 30 cm (12 in) between rows. The seed can be sown in early spring for summer varieties or later on in the summer for autumn and winter types. Turnips seem to taste better later in the year and as they are the kind of vegetable we tend to eat in the winter months, it's preferable to sow seed in the summer months rather than in the spring. Always check on your seed packet for variations.

When your seedlings are a few centimetres high, they should be thinned out to about 10–15 cm (4–6 in) between each one to allow root development. Again check on the manufacturer's growing recommendations for any variations. Make sure the ground is wet before you start and remove the weaker plants where possible. Firm down the remaining plants with your fingers very carefully and then water gently to allow any movement to settle. The thinnings or plants you pull out can be added to the salad bowl. They are very nutritious and it's a shame to discard them. Don't be tempted to transplant these seedlings; as with most root vegetables, they will fork or split and won't develop well.

ABOVE *Perfect turnips, ready to be used immediately or stored for later use – they keep very well for some months.*

Care and maintenance

Keep the ground watered, especially in long dry periods, and ensure the area is free from weeds. If your plants are allowed to dry out, they won't thrive, so water regularly.

Turnips are a brassica and are vulnerable to the same diseases as cabbages and other brassicas. Avoid club root by regulating acidic soil, as mentioned in the 'Gardener's Tip' on the opposite page, and also watch out for the cabbage white butterfly that will lay her eggs on the underside of your brassica leaves. Turnips are not immune to this butterfly and the resulting caterpillars can completely annihilate your crops in just a couple of days. Be vigilant. Check on the underside of the leaves every day as soon as you see the first cabbage white butterfly. Remove any eggs by scraping off or remove the whole leaf and compost.

Harvesting

Pull up a few turnips when they are quite small and enjoy these. Many vegetables are sweeter when young and can be freely enjoyed when you are growing your own. Don't pull them all when they are small, however, allow some to develop fully.

The leaves can also be used like spinach or swede leaves. Only take a few leaves from each plant or grow a variety specifically bred to produce plenty of foliage but not fully grown roots.

Storing

Turnips can be stored successfully in a vegetable clamp as described at the beginning of this chapter in Potatoes (see page 36). They will keep for many months in ideal conditions.

Laying turnips in boxes once they have been cleaned of soil is another storage option. Don't wash turnips; like other root vegetables, they will not keep if you do. Just dry the roots in the sun or a cool airy place, then brush off any excess soil. They should last quite well for a few weeks without wrinkling or drying out too much.

Turnips can also be frozen; cube and blanch in boiling water for five minutes then drain, cool and freeze quickly. Label the container or freezer bag. Or make a turnip soup, then blend and freeze.

Gardener's tip

Turnips are a member of the brassica family and are subject to the same diseases as cabbages and the like. Club root, which affects all brassicas can be avoided if the soil is not too acidic. Brassicas don't thrive well in very acid soil anyway, so check the pH before you start in order to make sure the ground is fairly neutral. Check on your seed packet for variations. Adjust if necessary with lime or other organic products a month or so before sowing.

Vitamins

Turnips are a good source of vitamin C, having around 11–12 mg per 100 g (4 oz). They are also very low in calories, making turnips an ideal vegetable in a calorie-controlled diet. A cooked turnip has only around 22 calories per 100 g (4 oz).

As with most root vegetables, turnips are a good source of minerals, including calcium and potassium, and dietary fibre – include this useful and tasty vegetable as often as possible in your winter diet.

Turnip greens are also rich in dietary fibre, minerals and vitamin C, as well as containing a significant amount of folate. However, turnip greens contain goitrogens and shouldn't be eaten by those with untreated thyroid conditions.

Recipe ideas

Turnips tend to be thought of as a boring vegetable with a rather bland taste but with a little inspiration in the kitchen they can be very tasty. This root is definitely worth eating for its nutritional value alone.

Turnip mash and rissoles

- Turnips can be mashed in the same way as potatoes and swede. Prepare turnips by peeling and cutting into fairly small pieces. Potatoes generally cook a bit quicker than turnips so if you want to cook them together in the same pan, cut the potatoes bigger than the turnip pieces.
- Put all prepared potatoes and turnips in a pan and cover with water. Bring to the boil then reduce heat and simmer until all vegetables are cooked through.
- Remove from the heat and drain well. Return to the pan and mash using a potato masher or a fork. Stir in a knob of butter, a little seasoning and a handful of chopped fresh herbs – sage and thyme work well with turnip. Stir well and serve immediately.
- Any leftovers can be stored in the fridge overnight and fried as turnip rissoles the next day. Shape the mixture into balls and flatten to make rissole shapes up to about an 25 mm (1 in) thick.
- Fry gently in a little olive oil on both sides for 5–10 minutes or until browned and hot right through. They can be baked on a baking sheet in a medium oven for about 20 minutes if preferred. Serve hot with a salad.

Crunchy turnip crumble

Boil, drain and mash 2 medium turnips. Mix together 1 tbsp brown sugar, 1 tsp baking powder, salt and pepper and a pinch of nutmeg. Add to the mashed turnips then place in an ovenproof dish. Toss 8 tbsp breadcrumbs with 2 tbsp melted butter and sprinkle on top of the turnip mixture. Bake in the oven for 20–25 minutes at 180°C (350°F/gas mark 4).

Creamy turnip gratin

Rub two small ramekin dishes with garlic and butter generously. Peel and thinly slice a medium turnip, parboil for 2 minutes and drain. Return to the pan and add 150 ml (5 fl oz) double cream, 1 tsp dried herbs and 50 g (2 oz) thinly sliced pancetta. Season and simmer until the turnip is tender. Spoon the mixture into the prepared ramekin dishes and warm in the oven until golden on top.

Other ideas

- Eat turnips raw, finely grated into salads.
- Roast in the same way as potatoes. They can also be cut into very thin matchsticks and stir fried.
- Grate into the sauce when you are making a lasagne, bolognaise or casserole dish.
- Make into a soup, along with carrot, potato and leeks if you have them to hand. Add a splash of cream when ready to serve.

Beetroot

Beetroot has been cultivated for many centuries, although before the 17th century it was grown mainly for its leaves in the kitchen garden; the roots were used for medicinal preparations (among other uses, beetroot was considered an effective aphrodisiac). It contains the element boron, which has since proven to have an effect on hormones.

The round purple-red root we eat today is just as nutritious as the leaves. If you like the idea of using beetroot leaves in place of spinach or other leafy greens, grow a line just for the foliage and another line for the roots.

It appears that beetroot was originally a seaside plant found over large coastal areas in Europe and Asia. The plant is well adapted to the vegetable garden and is probably one of the easier root crops to grow.

Seed

When you buy beetroot seeds, make sure you know what you're buying! Some beetroot seeds will be better for foliage than the roots. Try both if you have the space, or if you are only interested in the root crops, select a good cropping everyday beetroot to start with.

If you can't find a variety specifically for the foliage, grow a small line of any beetroot seed and use some of the plants for leaves and leave the rest to develop roots. When you remove leaves regularly the plant will produce more leaf and won't put energy into developing the root. The seeds are 'multiple' and will need thinning out later on, however thinly you sow.

It may be possible to sow the seed in individual biodegradable pots, but generally all root crops are better sown directly outside in the vegetable patch. If you transplant root crop seedlings, they tend to fork or split and won't develop into healthy roots. If you do try using biodegradable pots, remove the weaker seedlings to leave a strong seedling in each pot as soon as they are large enough to handle. Soak the soil with water first so you don't dislodge the plants you are leaving to grow on. Firm the soil gently round the plants after thinning and water gently.

Sowing

When sowing outdoors, prepare your soil first. Beetroot doesn't like an acidic soil, so check the pH levels of the soil if you aren't sure. If necessary add lime or any other organic material to rebalance the soil a month or so before sowing the seed.

Choose a sunny well-drained spot in the garden and dig over to a good depth. The cleaner and more

prepared your soil, the better your root crops will develop. Remove any perennial weeds, large stones and non-organic debris and then rake over the surface to a fine consistency for your seeds.

Seed should be sown after all danger of frost has passed. With a raised bed system and a plastic cloche-type covering, you could start beetroot seed a little earlier, but the seed won't germinate well if it's cold or doesn't have enough light. Sow seed thinly in shallow drills, preferably positioning one seed cluster every few centimentres or so, leaving about 30 cm (12 in) between rows. Cover with soil. Check the manufacturer's growing recommendations on your seed packet before you start for variety and regional variations. Water gently after sowing and keep the soil watered regularly in dry weather. Remove any weeds as they appear.

Care and maintenance

After a few weeks, your seedlings will need thinning out. Choose a wet day or soak the ground first with water. Gently remove weaker seedlings leaving 10–15 cm (4–6 in) of growing room for each plant. Again double-check on your seed packet for spacing advice. Firm the soil gently round the plants left in the ground. Water again if needed.

Keep beetroot plants healthy by watering regularly in dry weather and making sure they are weed-free. They are a hardy root crop and fairly resistant to bugs and disease, athough all young plants will need protection against slug and snail attacks.

Harvesting

The roots can be pulled and eaten as soon as they are golf-ball size. Make sure they are all collected before the first frost in the autumn or winter unless you have

ABOVE *Both leaves and roots of the beetroot can be eaten — cook tender young leaves at you would spinach.*

FAR LEFT *Harvest your beetroots before they get too large; loosen the soil around the root first, then pull out by the stems.*

ABOVE *Condition the soil well before sowing to ensure a good crop of beetroot, then sow in shallow drills.*

found a frost-resistant variety. Try not to leave them too long as they can become woody and lose some of their flavour. Collect when they are quite small if you intend to pickle them.

Use a fork to gently loosen the soil around each beetroot before you lift it to prevent any damage. Remove the leaves by twisting them rather than cutting through the root. Leaves should be collected regularly but never strip one plant of all its leaves. Take a few from each and the plants will stay healthy and crop for longer in the season.

Storing

Beetroot is generally stored in the form of pickled beetroot or it can be simply bottled as you would bottle any other vegetable. Bottling requires special equipment, but pickling can be done with just a large pan and some jars. See recipes opposite for a quick and easy way to pickle beetroot.

The roots can also be stored in the fridge for a week or so, or in a cool dark place for a few weeks. Keep an eye on them because they don't tend to store as well as other roots. Beetroot could also be stored in a vegetable clamp if you are using this method to store root crops (see page 36).

Vitamins

Beetroots are high in dietary fibre, folate and vitamin C, and the dark pigment actively helps fight free radicals in the body. Beetroots have been consumed in soup form for many years and are sometimes believed to be the secret ingredient to longevity. Packed with minerals and vitamins, beetroot is an excellent vegetable to include in a healthy diet. The high natural sugar levels make it one of the sweeter-tasting root vegetables, with an earthy after-taste.

Recipe ideas

Beetroot is traditionally pickled for winter storage, but there are so many other ways to enjoy this superfood in both sweet and savoury dishes. It is also delicious raw when grated over salads.

Beetroot and chocolate cake

Using beetroot in a cake may not seem like a good idea, but beetroot is actually very sweet and makes this delicious cake incredibly moist.

● Remove the leaves from 1 large beetroot and scrub clean. Put the beetroot in a pan, bring to the boil, then cover and simmer for 1–2 hours until tender. Leave to cool and then chop roughly.

● Preheat the oven to 190°C (375°F/gas mark 5). Tip the chopped beetroot into a food processor and blitz. Add a pinch of salt, 200 g (8 oz) plain flour, 100 g (4 oz) cocoa powder, 1 tbsp baking powder, 250 g (9 oz) golden caster sugar, 3 eggs and 2 tsp vanilla extract, then blitz again until completely mixed.

● Gradually add 200 ml (8 fl oz) sunflower oil in a steady stream, as if you were making mayonnaise. Once it has all been added, stir in 100 g (4 oz) dark chocolate pieces and tip into a loaf tin. Bake for an hour, or until a skewer comes out clean. Serve as an afternoon treat with crème fraîche or cream.

Tasty lamb burgers with beetroot relish

Burgers are an all-time favourite that the whole family will enjoy. These lamb burgers are succulent topped with a quick and nutritious relish.

● To make 4 burgers, finely dice 2 shallots and add half to a pan with a little olive oil and soften. Remove from the heat and leave to cool.

● In a separate bowl, place the remaining diced shallot, grate in 2 large raw beetroots, a splash of olive oil and a handful of chopped dill. Season, stir and set aside.

● Place 500 g (18 oz) lamb mince in a bowl, add the cooked shallot and a pinch of salt. Using your hands, knead the mixture well to combine, then shape into 4 burgers. Put on a plate and chill for 30 minutes.

● Preheat your grill and cook the burgers for about 5 minutes on each side. Serve in toasted burger buns topped with the beetroot relish and a green salad.

Quick beetroot and potato salad

Twist leaves off 4 medium beetroots, scrub and cook whole in boiling water until tender. Do the same with 4 medium potatoes. Leave to cool, then cut into cubes the same size and gently stir together in a bowl. Add 1 small red onion, finely diced. In a separate bowl mix together 150 ml (5 fl oz) natural yoghurt, a finely chopped green pepper and season. Stir most of the yoghurt mixture into the potatoes and beetroot, keeping a little aside to spoon over the top. Garnish with a few parsley leaves and chill for 10 minutes before serving.

Beetroot, horseradish and crème fraîche dip

Blitz 2 medium cooked beetroots, 2 tbsp horseradish sauce and 100 ml (4 fl oz) crème fraîche in a food processor. Season well, spoon into a bowl and serve with breadsticks, pitta breads or vegetable sticks. Whizzed up in minutes and with a hot horseradish kick, this dip is perfect for entertaining.

Other ideas

● Grate raw and stir into a green salad. Or use as a stand-alone salad with a squeeze of lemon juice, a pinch of ground cumin and a handful of sultanas.

● To pickle beetroot in jars, first prepare the jars by washing and rinsing well then dry in a very slow oven to sterilize. Use small beetroots for pickling, but don't cut before cooking as the roots 'bleed' and lose colour and goodness. Boil until tender then leave to cool slightly. Put as many beetroots as you can in each jar without damaging them and pour pickling vinegar over them. Seal the jars. Label and store out of direct light until needed.

Legumes

In a moderate climate the most widely grown plants of the legume family are peas and beans, and one of the more practical aspects of growing these two vegetables is that they will grow happily together. Legumes gather nitrogen from the air and take it down through the plant into the roots, which means that your pea and bean plants are nourishing the soil for next year's crops.

Other everyday legumes include peanuts and lentils, but these tend to grow successfully only in hotter climates. If you have a greenhouse, however, or live in a hotter part of the world there's no reason why you shouldn't try producing your own peanuts.

Beans

Beans make up a large group in the legume family, and come in all shapes and sizes — choose a variety that is suitable for your growing space and that you like to eat! Bush beans, French beans, broad beans and other similar varieties are easy to grow in moderate to cooler climates, but tend to be less hardy than peas. Although they need a warmer growing period, most like lots of rain. The beans we shell, such as butter beans and haricots need a longer growing season, but if you start them early and protect against cold nights, it's possible to grow these varieties in a cooler climate. Read the growing recommendations on the packet before you buy your seeds.

Green beans

Seed

As mentioned above, always check on the manufacturer's growing recommendations before you plant. Beans cover a lot of different varieties and it really is not worth trying to grow those types that will struggle to thrive. Because of their delicate root system, most beans are generally sown *in situ* as they don't transplant well. However, if you are trying one of the longer-growing varieties, you could start them early using biodegradable pots. Keep in a warm place before planting the whole pot outside later in the year.

Green beans also have different needs. Climbing varieties need a support system and this should·be constructed before you sow your seed. Choose a sunny spot in the garden. Peas and beans grow well together in the same plot, so although beans are usually planted later in the year, they can still occupy the same space.

Sowing

Dig over the ground and remove any perennial weeds, large stones and non-organic debris before raking over to a fine consistency. Set up any support structure you need at this point. Low-growing bush varieties won't need any support at all, but taller growing or climbing plants will need something. A popular way to grow runner beans is in a tepee design.

Push long canes into the ground firmly in a circle. They should be about 1.8 m (6 ft) high when in place. Then bring the tops of the canes together and tie firmly with garden twine to form a tepee shape. Attach strings around the canes every 20–25 cm (8–10 in) starting from about 15 cm (6 in) above the ground and carry on until you get to the top of the tepee. Make sure the strings are taut and securely attached, as your

RIGHT *Beans come in many different varieties and types — and thrive in many climates. Both French and broad beans (inset) do very well under moderate to cool conditions.*

ABOVE *Keep your young bean plants warm – you can use old window frames as here or whatever you have to hand.*

plants will use these for support. If you decide this design isn't suitable for your garden, beans can be trained up a sunny fence or any other structure.

Beans should be sown in drills about 2.5–5 cm (1–2 in) deep and about 5–7.5 cm (2–3 in) apart. If you are planting bush varieties in lines, allow 15–30 cm (6–12 in) between the seeds and 45–60 cm (18–24 in) between the rows. Bush varieties are often very heavy cropping plants and it's a good idea to sow a line every

two or three weeks through the spring and early summer for a constant supply rather than having too many beans at once.

Care and maintenance

Keep the young plants watered and weed-free. Beans have a fairly delicate root structure and hoeing should be done very gently. It's preferable to hand-weed where possible. Runner bean flowers should be sprayed with water twice a day if the weather is dry, to 'set' the flowers. If the plants are lacking water the flowers will drop before the pods have formed. Other varieties will need watering regularly but not necessarily as often as runner beans. Double-check on your seed packet for manufacturer's watering recommendations.

Harvesting

Pick your beans as soon as they are ready. Try not to leave them on the plant too long as they can become stringy, unless you are growing butter beans or another variety where you discard the pod before eating. Generally you would leave these varieties on the plant until fully developed, but make sure the autumn rains or cold nights aren't too harsh or the plants will start to rot. Harvest early if you think the weather is about to turn nasty.

All green beans should be eaten when they are small and tender for the best flavour and nutritional value. Green beans are particularly heavy cropping plants and you shouldn't deny yourself a treat of young beans as soon as you can. French beans should be several centimetres long or more before you eat them.

As with peas, leave the plants in the ground to completely die back, then dig into the soil to nourish the ground for next year's crops, or cut down to ground level and leave them to rot into the soil.

Broad beans

Seed

Broad beans are a good cool climate crop and can be sown in either autumn or early spring. Many growers prefer to start broad bean in autumn as they are less likely to be attacked by black fly. Broad beans are especially vulnerable to this pest although nipping the top off the plant sometimes helps deter it.

If you are sowing your seed in the autumn, choose as sheltered and bright a spot as possible. A support structure is preferable, as you can protect your plants from winter winds by tying them firmly to the support. Push two fairly long, strong canes or sticks into the ground at either end of the row and join them with a couple of cross beams or string. Use wooden slats or more canes or sticks and tie firmly together. If the structure is weak it can be counter-productive as the wind may blow it down taking your plants with it.

Sowing

Once you have your structure in place sow seed every few centimetres. Check the manufacturer's sowing recommendations before you start. Sow about 2.5–5 cm (1–2 in) deep and water well. Make sure your plants get enough water in the first few weeks especially. Broad beans grown through the winter months tend to get enough rainfall to thrive.

Care and maintenance

Keep an eye on your plants until they get established and watch out for slug and snail attacks. If you are spring sowing, your broad beans may not need support although check the guidance and instructions.

ABOVE *These flowering broad bean plants are supported by rows of string tied to canes at either end of the row.*

Harvesting

Broad beans should be picked as soon as the beans inside the pods start to swell. The pods do grow fairly large and can sometimes be deceptive, so give the beans enough time to develop fully, but try not to leave them on the plant to get too old. Young broad beans are a particularly delicious treat.

Storing

There are many different types of beans so the storing methods are quite varied. French beans, runner beans and any complete pod green bean can be frozen. Blanch in boiling water for 5 minutes, drain and cool completely. Freeze quickly to limit the loss of colour, nutritional value and taste. They can also be bottled very successfully. Try this method if you are set up with home bottling equipment.

The beans that we shell before eating, such as butter beans, broad beans and kidney beans can be dried for storing. They store almost indefinitely in the right conditions. Shell the beans, remove any damaged ones and blanch for 5 or 10 minutes in boiling water. Remove from heat, drain and leave to cool. Spread the beans out in single layers on baking trays and heat in a very slow oven set at the lowest temperature for a few hours, turning every half hour or so. When they are completely dry, leave to cool then store in sealable jars out of direct light. Peas and beans tend to keep for a long time, so it is best to date them in order that you always use the oldest ones first.

After blanching, broad beans can also be frozen quickly and stored for several months in the freezer.

Vitamins

Beans are a good source of protein, dietary fibre, calcium and vitamins A and C. They should always be cooked before eating as they contain a toxin that is harmful in their raw state. Once cooked, beans are perfectly safe to eat, of course. Cooked green beans can actually aid digestion and are safe to eat every day. After cooking, retain the water as this will contain iron from the beans and can be used to make gravy or sauces.

Recipe ideas

Beans are really versatile in the kitchen and can be used in so many different ways. Remember to store some for the winter months.

Green bean and feta salad

Always cook beans before eating them. Don't be tempted to throw them in the salad bowl raw, however harmless they look. They do contain a toxin that needs to be cooked out first to make them safe to eat.

- Once your beans are prepared, cover with water in a saucepan. Bring to the boil, reduce heat and simmer until just cooked. Drain and cool completely.
- Shred a few lettuce leaves and put into a salad bowl, stir in the beans. Crumble a little feta cheese and stir through the salad together with a handful of black pitted olives. Dress with vinaigrette or serve separately.
- To make a simple dressing at home: put a tablespoon or two of white wine vinegar in a small bowl and add salt and pepper and a spoonful of Dijon or other prepared mustard. Mix well. Just before serving, stir in a tablespoon or two of olive oil and whisk quickly with a fork or a hand whisk. Serve immediately.

Creamy green beans

- Prepare and cook your beans. Drain well and leave to cool. In a large wok or frying pan, heat a little cooking oil or butter and gently cook about 85 g (3 oz) flaked or sliced almonds. You could also use mushrooms, cut into slices.
- Add the beans to the pan with a teaspoon or two fresh chopped oregano. Stir well and cook gently for a couple of minutes until thoroughly heated. Stir in a few tablespoons of sour cream or crème fraîche if preferred. Remove from the heat and serve hot.

Green bean and Stilton bake
- Preheat the oven to 200°C (400°F/gas mark 6). Blanch 250 g (9 oz) green beans in boiling water for about 3 minutes. Drain well and transfer to a lightly buttered casserole dish.
- Pour over 284 ml (10 fl oz) single cream and crumble over 50 g (2 oz) Stilton (or other blue cheese).
- In a food processor, blitz 2 slices wholemeal bread (crusts removed) to make breadcrumbs. Mix the breadcrumbs with 2 tbsp melted butter and sprinkle evenly over the top.
- Put in the oven and cook for around 15 minutes until browned.

Broad bean pesto
This rustic pesto recipe uses broad beans in place of the more traditional pine nuts and is really delicious tossed with warm pasta, potatoes or fish.
- In a food processor blitz 200 g (8 oz) cooked broad beans (boiled for 10 minutes and grey outer skins removed), 2 garlic cloves, large bunch fresh basil, 4 tbsp grated Parmesan, juice and zest of half a lemon, 2 tbsp olive oil and salt and pepper. Blitz until blended into a paste. This pesto can be stored in the refrigerator for up to a week.

Broad bean and prawn pilau
- Finely chop a large onion and 2 garlic cloves. Fry in a pan with a little oil along with 1 tsp turmeric and 1 tsp ground cumin until the onion is soft.
- Stir in 200 g (8 oz) basmati rice and cook for a further minute. Add 600 ml (1 pt) water, season and bring to the boil.
- Next add 250 g (9 oz) broad beans and simmer for 15 minutes. After this time, add 250g (9 oz) shelled and cooked prawns and simmer for another 5 minutes or so until the broad beans are tender and all the water has

been absorbed by the rice. Stir in a handful of chopped fresh coriander and leave to stand for a couple of minutes. Serve with crusty bread or a green salad.

Broad bean dip
This tasty dip is perfect for a quick, healthy lunch or snack. Spread on crusty bread or dip with carrot sticks.
- Simply shell broad beans, cover with water and bring to the boil. Reduce heat and simmer until beans are tender. Drain well and leave to cool completely.
- Tip into a food processor and blend until smooth, mixing in a little olive oil to make the mixture smoother. Add a clove of crushed garlic, some chopped parsley, then season and blend together until smooth.

Other ideas
- Boil or steam broad beans and serve as a side dish to any meal. They can be tossed with a knob of butter, black pepper or any other seasoning you prefer.
- Use in soups and stir frys.
- Haricots and other beans grown for the 'seed' part rather than the pod, make an excellent substitute for meat in lasagne, bolognaise or chilli dishes. Once cooked, they can be mashed into a paste and used in place of minced beef. Add a few finely chopped onions, herbs and spices and form into burger shapes for homemade organic veggie burgers. Or stir in a tin of chopped tomatoes and make a bolognaise dish as you would with minced beef.

Peas

Peas have been grown commercially for many years, but there is still nothing like a home-grown pea collected from your own patch. There are different varieties available and you should check carefully before buying seeds. Mange tout or sugar snap types are eaten before the peas inside the pod develop, and the whole pod can be eaten raw or cooked.

Everyday garden peas take a little longer to develop but are worth growing, and kids will love shelling the peas. Try a few different varieties if you have the space. They are generally planted quite early in the year so will be out of the way by later in the summer.

Seed

Peas, like beans are normally sown directly outside. It may be possible to start some varieties off in individual biodegradable pots, but most are fairly hardy and are better sown *in situ* wherever possible.

Generally, pea seeds are sown fairly early in the growing season – double-check the instructions on your seed packet for time differences and variations though. There are bush and vine varieties available, and both will grow well in a moderate climate. The vine varieties produce tendrils that will cling to a fence or other support system. Build your structure before you plant the seed to avoid any damage to the seed, root system or the young plants.

A length of pig wire stretched between two posts firmly pushed into the ground works well for peas, although there are all sorts of pea netting and trellis structures you can buy from garden suppliers. Bush varieties may need a cane or pea stick to help support them, particularly in windy areas. Pea sticks can be made from tree prunings, traditionally hazel. A thin branch with a couple of smaller branches leading from it works very well as a pea support.

Sowing

Choose a bright sunny spot in the garden, and ensure the ground is well drained. Dig over and remove any perennial weeds, large stones or non-organic debris and rake over to a fine consistency. Don't be tempted to add nitrates to your soil. Legumes catch nitrogen from the air and nourish the soil without you doing a thing. Sow your seeds 2.5–5 cm (1–2 in) deep, leaving a few centimetres between each one and about 60 cm (2 ft) between rows. Immediately after sowing, water well. Water regularly if the weather is particularly dry, although since peas are generally sown in the early spring, they do tend to get enough rainwater. Keep the weeds away and seeds should germinate within a couple of weeks.

ABOVE *Most pea varieties require some form of support – twigs, stakes and netting all work well.*

Care and maintenance

When the plants are quite small they will start to produce tendrils (in the vine varieties). Watch out for these and gently curl them round the support system you have in place. After the first one is done on each plant, they will find their own way, but keep an eye on them in case one or two get lost.

Don't mulch around pea plants as the stems can easily rot. They are a cool-climate crop so won't need pampering too much. Peas can be grown in containers although generally a support system needs to be in place, so the containers may need to be quite large to accommodate a pea stick as well as a plant.

Harvesting

Mange tout and sugar snap peas should be harvested as soon as the pods are a few centimetres long. They will keep on cropping so don't wait for them to grow any bigger. If you do miss a few, pull the strings off both sides of the pod and slice to add to a stir fry or eat raw.

Everyday garden peas should be collected when the pods are obviously swollen with peas inside. Again don't leave them too long. One of the nicest things about growing your own vegetables is that you can afford to eat them at their best, so don't miss this one.

Marrowfat peas should be left longer until fully mature, although always check on the seed packet for any variations.

If you are saving peas to dry, leave them on the plant until the pods start to split. Although it may be tempting to leave the last ones that grow to dry, it's better to save a few of the earlier pods so they have longer to develop and dry naturally on the plant.

Leave the plants to die back on their own. Try not to pull them up while tidying the space. If you leave them to die back naturally then dig them into the soil, you are replenishing the ground and the area will be more fertile for next year's crops. Or, alternatively, cut the plant down to ground level and leave the roots to rot away into the soil.

Storing

Peas can be frozen for up to a year. Freeze quickly in single layers, then bag and label. They can also be bottled if you have the right equipment. Probably the easiest method, though, is to store them as dried peas. Leave the pods to dry as much as possible on the plant, and collect when the pods begin to split naturally. Harvest all of the pods before the autumn rains and cold nights arrive.

Some peas may have holes in them where worms have eaten through the pod. Rather than picking them all over, the best thing to do is to put a handful of peas at a time in a bowl of cold water. The ones that rise to the top have air-holes in them and have had worms burrowing into them.

Shell peas and blanch for a few minutes in boiling water. Drain and leave to cool completely. Lay on baking sheets and heat in a very cool oven (set at its lowest temperature) until completely dry. Turn every half an hour or so. When dry, leave to cool, then store in airtight jars out of direct light. Peas dried in this way will keep almost indefinitely.

In general, fresh vegetables tend to be more nutritious as they still have all the enzymes that are inevitably reduced during the process of drying or freezing. However, quickly freezing vegetables such as peas as soon as they are picked will help to retain their goodness. Store in plastic freezer bags and label them with dates and variety.

Vitamins

Peas are a good source of vitamins A and C, which are both antioxidants and will help fight free radicals in the body. Niacin is also present, which helps with the absorption of iron. They are easy to digest and are often served as a side vegetable to those recovering from illness. They are also believed to protect the body against many ageing conditions, so they could, in fact, help you live longer.

BELOW *Dried split peas are delicious and filling when made into hearty winter soups and stews.*

Recipe ideas

Pea and mint soup

Traditionally, pea soup would be bubbling away on the stove for days, with more ingredients added when available. This recipe is simple and quick to make and really is a tasty treat for early summer or for later in the year. You can use dried peas instead of fresh, but soak overnight in water before using. They will take longer to cook than fresh green peas.

● Melt a little butter and add a finely diced onion to the pan. Cook until soft then add about 1 litre (2 pt) vegetable or chicken stock and about 1 kg (2.2 lbs) peas. Stir in a handful of chopped fresh mint and season to taste. Bring to the boil, then reduce heat and simmer for 30–40 minutes or until the peas are tender.

● Remove from the heat and allow to cool slightly. Then blend in a liquidizer or food processor until smooth. Return to the pan and very gently heat through, stirring all the time.

● Serve hot in individual bowls with a swirl of single cream and a couple of mint leaves to garnish.

Basil, pea and pancetta tart

Another great recipe for feeding the whole family or for when you're having guests. Using a ready-made pastry case makes this dish quick and easy to rustle up, and can easily be prepared the day before you want to serve it.

● Bring a 284 ml (10 fl oz) pot of double cream to the boil, then remove from the heat and add a small bunch of fresh basil. Leave to infuse for an hour.

● Blanch 100 g (4 oz) fresh or frozen peas in a pan of boiling water for 1 minute, drain and cool quickly under the cold tap. Heat the grill and cook 6 slices pancetta until crisp and drain on kitchen paper.

● Heat the oven to 180°C (350°F/gas mark 4). Strain the cream into a bowl through a sieve, then beat in 3 eggs plus 1 yolk, a handful of grated Parmesan and season. Tear the pancetta into small pieces and sprinkle into the pastry case along with the peas. Pour in the egg and cream mix – there may be a little of the mixture left depending on the size of your pastry case.

● Bake for around 50 minutes until set in the middle. You can serve this tart hot or cold, and it is delicious with shavings of Parmesan on top.

Lemony pea risotto

This risotto couldn't be simpler and is a quick supper to rustle up after a day at work or in the garden.

● In a large saucepan, heat a little olive oil and stir in 200 g (8 oz) Arborio (risotto) rice for a minute, stirring constantly. Gradually add a ladleful at a time of 850 ml (28 fl oz) hot vegetable stock until the rice is almost cooked and all the stock is absorbed. This will take about 20 minutes.

● Add 50 g (2 oz) peas (fresh or frozen), cook for a further 5 minutes then remove from the heat. Stir in a handful of grated Parmesan, the juice and zest of half a lemon and season.

● Serve immediately, with lemon zest and Parmesan scattered on top.

Stir-fried beef with mange tout

One of the tastiest ways to serve mange tout is in a stir fry. Be careful not to cook them for more than a couple of minutes though, otherwise they will lose their colour and crispness.

● Marinate 200 g (8 oz) finely sliced rump steak with 1 tbsp Chinese rice wine (or dry sherry), 1 tsp cornflour and 2 tbsp oyster sauce for 20 minutes.

● In a wok, heat a little groundnut oil and add 2 coarsely sliced spring onions and 1 tsp finely chopped fresh ginger. Stir fry for a minute then add the beef, stirring for a further 2 minutes until browned. Set to one side in a warm bowl.

● Add a little more oil to the wok and stir fry the mange tout for 2 minutes along with a pinch of salt and sugar. Return the beef to the wok, toss everything together and serve with steamed rice.

Other ideas

● When the peas have swollen in the pods, collect from the plants and get everyone to help with the shelling ritual. It's great fun! Shell peas, removing any damaged or worm-infested ones. Put the shells and damaged ones on the compost heap. Gently rinse the peas and put into a pan. Cover with water and bring to the boil. Reduce heat and simmer until peas are tender. This usually takes 15–20 minutes, depending on the size of the peas. A mint leaf or two can be added to the pan if liked. Or after the peas have cooked, drain well, return to the pan and stir in a knob of butter and a few freshly chopped mint leaves. Perfect with new potatoes and a Sunday roast.

● Chop mange tout pods and toss into a bowl of green salad. The crisp, fresh sweetness of the pea pods brings alive all the other flavours in your salad. They can also be sliced lengthwise and mixed into any number of stir-fry dishes.

● Add peas to many dishes to add bulk, colour, flavour and nutrition.

● Try them in Spanish omelettes – cook peas, cool and drain and add with the other vegetables to your egg mixture before cooking.

● Add to rice salad – cook first, drain and leave until completely cold. Stir into a dish of cold cooked rice with finely chopped onion and a red pepper. Season and add a squeeze of lemon.

Green vegetables

There are many leafy green vegetables that can be grown right through the winter months. It is important to include leafy vegetables in our diets as they are full of vitamins that help prevent colds and flu during the colder months of the year. And when you pick and eat them fresh, the goodness is still locked in, allowing you to eat the most nutritious foods possible. Brussels sprouts, for instance, can be collected with little caps of snow on them and are really delicious straight from the garden, whatever anyone says about 'hating sprouts'!

As well as the green vegetables listed here, winter cabbage and spring greens are others you might like to try growing. Plan to sow a few lines of late seed after the summer crops have finished so you keep your garden producing food for as many months of the year as possible.

Kale

Kale is a hardy green vegetable that will put up with almost anything the weather throws at it. It grows well in northern climates and is a popular vegetable in many places. Kale is a primitive cabbage and has been cultivated for thousands of years, proving itself to be a useful winter crop. It is a biennial plant, producing foliage in the first year and flower and seed in the second year of growth. A nutritious leafy green crop, kale is a delight to pick fresh from the garden during the winter months and even nicer to eat during this time when many green summer vegetables are unavailable.

Seed

There are a number of different types of kale including the curly variety that is often found in supermarkets. It's also possible to buy an ornamental variety, which can be used as a garnish but not eaten as a green vegetable, so double-check to see which variety you are buying.

Kale is a brassica like cabbage and the seed can be sown directly outside or started indoors. Seed should be sown in trays or pots in early spring for summer cropping, or outside in the summer for winter crops. Check on the seed packet for early and late sowing recommendations.

Sowing and planting out

Sow in well-drained trays or pots of fresh compost and keep fairly warm and water regularly. Seeds should germinate in 10–14 days. Thin seedlings when they are large enough to handle leaving the strongest one in each pot to grow on. Make sure the soil is damp before you start the thinning-out process.

Try to keep your kale plants until the last of the pea plants have been dug back into the soil. Then loosen the top of the soil with a fork or spade, but don't dig again. Plant out the kale plants allowing about 45 cm (18 in) between each plant and 45 cm (18 in) between each row, in order to allow them space to develop. Water and keep the weeds at bay, especially in the early stages of growing. They don't have to be planted where the peas were, but they will benefit from the nitrates in the soil that will have been fixed there by the peas.

Kale seed can also be sown *in situ*. Because kale is a winter crop it doesn't really need to be sown until the summer. It should be sown thinly in shallow drills in a sunny well-drained spot in the garden. Only dig over the soil if it hasn't yet been worked earlier in the year. Keep weed-free and water regularly. Thin out seedlings to allow about 45 cm (18 in) between each plant.

Care and maintenance

Kale is one of the more accommodating brassicas and will thrive in most soils, although it's always better not to have too high an acid content. If you suspect your soil may be on the acidic side, neutralize with an organic product a month or so before planting.

Kale is a hardy plant and fairly resistant to bugs and viruses. However, if you are growing early crops, watch out for cabbage white butterflies. Kale is part of the brassica family and is a prime target for this butterfly. Check the undersides of the leaves every day if you've spotted the cabbage white butterfly at all in your garden. Scrape off any eggs or remove the whole leaf and compost it.

Make sure your plants don't dry out in the summer months. As autumn approaches, it's advisable in very windy areas to firm down the plants, and earth up the stems to protect the roots from too much ground frost. Check on your seed packet for other growing recommendations, as different varieties will have different requirements. Be sure to remove any yellowing leaves and keep free from weeds.

Harvesting

Early grown kale can be used as soon as the leaves become available. The plants can be cut down in late summer and may grow new shoots that you can collect in the winter months. There may be information on your seed packet about harvesting your variety of kale.

From around late autumn onwards, start cutting kale leaves for use in the kitchen. Never use yellowing or older leaves as they will taste bitter. Take the first leaves from the crown of the plant and only take a few leaves from each plant at a time. This will encourage

LEFT *All brassicas, including kale, are prone to caterpillar infestations. Check the undersides of leaves every day.*

the plant to produce new shoots from the main stem. The majority of your crop will come from these new shoots and will be ready to use from midwinter on into early spring. Cut the leaves with a sharp knife, or pull each leaf downwards, steadying the rest of the plant as you pull.

Storing

Because kale crops right through the winter months, there is very little need to store it. It will keep for a couple of days in the salad compartment of the fridge, but does tend to become more bitter in flavour the longer you keep it, so eat fresh wherever possible. Kale is a cold winter vegetable and will go limp very quickly in a warm kitchen. Don't wash the leaves before you put them in the fridge.

Vitamins

Kale is absolutely packed with goodness. It is an excellent source of vitamin C and many of the B vitamins. Fresh kale also contains plenty of calcium and folate as well as dietary fibre. It is particularly high in potassium with 228 mg per 100 g (4 oz), which is a vital mineral for many important functions in the body.

The edible plants in the brassica family are known as cruciferous vegetables, which have been shown to reduce the risk of certain cancers, and recent research indicates that they may help to reduce the risk of heart disease as well – a good reason in itself to make kale one of your five-a-day.

Recipe ideas

Green vegetables often takes a back seat when it comes to imaginative flair in the kitchen. It's all too easy to dish up as a second veg and then go through the process of convincing everyone to 'eat up their greens'. With a little creativity though, kale can be jazzed up so that everyone will want seconds. Not only do you get to feed the family on tasty and nutritious food, you can also enjoy your own dinner without having to moan at the kids! Try these ideas and invent a few of your own.

Mediterranean kale

Lemon juice gives kale a distinct Mediterranean taste.
● Make a dressing with olive or nut oil, a little salt and black pepper to taste and freshly squeezed lemon juice. Rinse kale then cut into strips and put into a large pan.
● Cover with water and bring to the boil. Reduce heat and simmer for 10 minutes or so until just cooked. Drain, then toss with the dressing.
● Other ingredients can be added if available. A clove or two of crushed garlic, some crumbled feta cheese and halved olives all add to the Mediterranean taste.

Kale pasta with chilli and anchovy

● In a large pan, boil some penne or other tubular pasta. While it's cooking, heat 2 tbsp olive oil in a saucepan, then sizzle a finely sliced red chilli, 2 chopped garlic cloves and 4 finely chopped anchovies. Add shredded kale, then gently fry until tender, adding a drop of water if needed.
● Drain the pasta, reserving a few tablespoons of the cooking water, then toss the pasta and water through the kale, adding 2 further tbsp olive oil, juice of half a lemon and grated Parmesan. Serve scattered with Parmesan shavings.

Kale, pumpkin and bacon hot-pot

Make a tasty stew that will warm the family on a cold winter's day. There are endless recipes for stews and hot-pots, but this one is simple to make and will appeal to all – you can use whatever you have available. Potatoes, leeks, carrots, parsnips and turnips, along with a chopped onion or two are all good vegetables to add to this stew.
● Fry a pack of finely chopped streaky bacon in a medium saucepan until crisp – you shouldn't need any oil as the bacon fat will melt quickly.
● Peel and chop one medium pumpkin into small cubes and add to the pan with 3 halved shallots. Fry until the edges start to brown, then add enough chicken or vegetable stock to cover and bring to a simmer. Cover and cook for 15 minutes or until the pumpkin is tender.
● Stir in 200 g (8 oz) chopped kale, cover and cook for about 5 minutes or until tender. Stir in a handful of freshly chopped parsley and season well. Serve with toasted crusty bread.

Other ideas

● Serve as a side vegetable to meat or fish dishes – either boiled, steamed, stir-fried or braised.
● Add to soups and casseroles to add bulk, flavour and plenty of nutrition.
● Finely slice and use as filling for a quiche or calzone.

Brussels sprouts

Sprouts are notoriously difficult to include in a family diet, as there is always at least one person who declares passionately that they hate sprouts. However, don't let that put you off. Sprouts grown in your own vegetable plot are very different from those you buy.

They are a hardy winter vegetable and will grow happily in very cold temperatures. I once tried to grow them in France but the winter wasn't cold enough for them to develop into hard sprouts. The plants grew well and produced tiny lettuce-like growths on the main stem, which were delicious. I managed to get the kids to eat them by telling them it was a variety of spinach!

Brussels sprouts seem to have originated in Europe and although they are very defined miniature cabbages, they haven't been cultivated for much longer than a few hundred years in kitchen gardens. Cabbages, on the other hand, have a much longer history and appear in records dating back thousands of years.

Seed

Sprouts are a long-growing, cool climate vegetable and seed should be sown around early to mid spring. If the ground is prepared and not too cold, seed can be sown outside *in situ* – check the manufacturer's growing recommendations on your seed packet before you start to sow. Plants tend to develop a healthier and stronger root system if they are planted *in situ* and do not suffer the trauma of being transplanted. However, if you sow the seed in biodegradable pots it shouldn't make too much difference overall. Plant the entire pot into the soil and the pot will disintegrate into the ground.

Sowing and planting out

Sow seed in well-drained trays, pots or biodegradable pots, in fresh compost. Keep protected and fairly warm, but not necessarily in a hothouse temperature. Water regularly. When seedlings are large enough to handle, thin to allow one plant per pot in biodegradable pots, or if you are transplanting later, 2 or 3 plants per pot can be allowed to grow on.

Seed sown directly outside should be sown after all danger of frost has passed in a well-prepared and well-drained bed in a sunny spot. As with all brassicas, sprouts don't thrive in an acidic soil, so make any adjustments in the month or two before sowing if necessary. Sow seed thinly in shallow drills. Water carefully and keep weed free. The seedlings should be thinned to allow about 10 cm (4 in) of growing space per plant. After a few more weeks, thin again to allow about 45 cm (18 in) between plants.

Although they are a hardy crop, young plants shouldn't be put outside until all danger of frost has

ABOVE *These brassica seedlings have been sown in open ground and will need thinning out.*

passed, usually around mid to late spring in cooler climates. When your plants are 20–30 cm (8–12 in) high, they can be transplanted to the garden or large containers outside. There's no need to over-protect sprout plants. Keeping them too warm is counter-productive as they prefer a cool growing climate.

It's a good idea to choose a fairly firm soil and put a stake in the ground just before planting. Brussels sprout plants are top-heavy and can get blown down in strong winds. Tie the plants to the stakes as they get bigger. Use garden twine and allow room for the stem to grow. Allow 45 cm (18 in) between plants and between rows and plant carefully. Biodegradable pots can be planted without disturbing the plant, but water well to give the roots a chance to break through the pot.

Care and maintenance

Make sure your plants don't get bogged down with weeds. In late spring and early summer, weeds can take over in a few days, so keep an eye on your crops. Remove weeds by hand wherever possible, as the plants have shallow root systems and can be damaged by hoes or trowels.

Brussels sprouts are not immune to the cabbage white butterfly, so look out for this pest. Another problem sprout plants can suffer from when they are very small and vulnerable is slug and snail attacks. These creatures will attack any young plants and can eat through the stems of a whole row of plants in one sitting so watch out for them. However, overall sprouts tend to be pretty hardy plants and will resist most diseases. Try not to let your plants dry out in a hot summer. If you find the ground is drying out too much, shade the plants as much as you can during the hottest part of the day.

Harvesting

A healthy plant in ideal conditions can produce around a 1 kg (2.2 lb) sprouts. If you find the sprouts don't form into complete, round, hard little cabbages, don't worry. They are still edible and you may be able to get away with convincing 'sprout-hating' members of the family that these are not even sprouts at all!

Pick Brussels sprouts as soon as they are ready. Pull each one off the stem or cut with a sharp knife. The top leaves of the plant can also be cooked and eaten as early spring greens. Sprouts will often crop from midwinter right through until early spring, depending on the variety and the weather conditions. In ideal conditions, the plant may develop more sprouts after you have picked some of them. Try not to strip a whole plant in one go and you may be rewarded with a second crop.

Storing

Brussels sprouts are another cold weather crop that can usually be left in the ground safely throughout the winter months, so you can pick as and when you need them. They do, however, freeze quite successfully. Remove any damaged parts then blanch in boiling water for five minutes. Drain well and cool completely. Put into labelled containers or freezer bags and store in the freezer. Sprouts will also keep in a cool place or in the salad compartment of the fridge for a few days.

Vitamins

Brussels sprouts contain the same goodness as kale, in slightly different quantities. They are a good source of vitamins C and B as well as being high in potassium. They are also a good source of folate and calcium. Their vitamin content will help ward off winter colds and flu and will help boost the immune system. All cruciferous vegetables (edible brassicas) may help prevent certain cancers and generally improve your health and that of your family.

BELOW *Heavily laden Brussels sprouts plants ready for use; pick the individual sprouts as soon as they are ready.*

Recipe ideas

The secret to the best-tasting Brussels sprouts is simple – do not overcook them. Sprouts actually release a sulphur-type chemical when overcooked, which makes them taste very bitter. Be imaginative in the way you prepare and serve your sprouts. Use nut oil to cook or dress them, or mix with nuts or other green vegetables. Once cooked they can be chopped or even mashed and mixed with other vegetables, including roots such as potatoes or turnips. Or add a few leftover sprouts to soups, stews and casseroles. The liquid used to cook sprouts can be added to soups and stews so you get an even bigger dose of vitamins.

Sprouts and chestnuts

Sprouts and chestnuts is a classic combination for Christmas dinner. Nuts complement green vegetables really well, but roasted or boiled chestnuts stirred in with a bowl of steaming sprouts is something special.
- Prepare your sprouts by removing any damaged or coarse outer leaves. Put in a pan and cover with water. Bring to the boil, reduce the heat and simmer until the sprouts are just cooked. Drain well.
- At the same time or before, cook your chestnuts. Either peel and roast them or boil until tender. Stir the chestnuts and sprouts together in a serving dish and top with a knob of butter. Serve hot.

Bubble and Squeak

Any greens, including sprouts, can be used to make the traditional bubble and squeak.
- Use leftovers if you have any, otherwise cook the sprouts first then chop finely and stir into a bowl of mashed potato. Add seasoning and fresh herbs to taste.
- Put the mixture into a frying pan with a little heated sunflower or olive oil. Cook gently so that a golden crust forms on both sides.
- If you prefer, the mixture can be formed into individual-sized cakes before cooking. Roll into balls and flatten them slightly before popping them into the frying pan. Or they can be baked on a sheet in a preheated oven for 20 minutes or so until golden.

Stir fry

Sprouts taste delicious stir-fried. Choose smaller ones if possible or cut larger ones in half lengthwise. Boil the sprouts first, drain well then add to the other stir-fry vegetables in your pan or wok. Heat gently until hot right through. Serve immediately. Use a splash of nut or olive oil to stir-fry your vegetables. You can also shread the sprouts before adding them to your stir fry, in which case you won't have to boil them beforehand.

Other ideas

- Brussels sprouts can be steamed as well as boiled.
- Fry cooked sprouts in a pan with salty pancetta or bacon pieces.
- Add grated or chopped and cooked sprouts to mashed potato with a sprinkling of Parmesan for an unusual twist on cheesy mash.
- Brussels sprouts make a surprisingly good purée – blitz boiled or steamed sprouts in a food processor with a touch of single cream, season well with pepper and salt and perhaps a little grated nutmeg.

Winter lettuce

Winter lettuces are fun to grow and bring a touch of summer to the cold weather meals. Some of the Chinese leaf varieties can be planted late in the summer months for autumn picking. These are known as Chinese cabbage, Chinese leaf or Chinese lettuce. Check on seed packets for variations. There are literally hundreds of different types of lettuce so double-check that you are buying the ones you want.

Winter lettuce is often very simple and straightforward to grow, and is sadly neglected as a winter crop. Although we don't tend to eat cold foods so often in the winter, there is nothing quite like the taste of a fresh green salad at any time of the year and often winter lettuce is slightly sweeter-tasting than the summer varieties. Unless you are intending to eat a lot of winter salad, a few healthy plants will probably be all you need to see you through.

Seed

Choose your seed carefully. There are some lettuce varieties that are suitable for all year growing, although they may need a little extra protection during the colder months of the year. It's a good idea to have a small cloche available to protect all young plants during cold weather, especially frosty nights.

Experiment with a couple of lettuce varieties if you have the space. The cut-and-come-again types are loose-leafed and you can steal a few leaves from the plants every few days. Arctic King and other winter lettuces can be grown successfully outside in cool climates, although they may need a little overnight protection during the coldest parts of the year.

Sowing and planting out

Sow the seed from late summer to late autumn. If you are sowing directly outside, sow sooner rather than later to avoid frost damage to seedlings. Prepare well-drained pots or trays with fresh compost and sow seed thinly. Keep warm and watered.

Prepare a sunny well-drained spot in the garden. Choose a sheltered area if possible to protect your plants from cold winds in the winter months. Dig over the ground lightly, and incorporate some well-rotted compost to feed the soil if necessary. Plant out seedlings when they are large enough to handle and allow about 30 cm (12 in) all round for the lettuce to

fully develop. Double-check the manufacturer's recommendations on your seed packets, as varieties differ in their spacing requirements.

Seed should be sown as thinly as possible in shallow drills. Sow short lines of winter lettuce seed every couple of weeks or so from late summer to late autumn. Water well after sowing and then regularly until later in the year when the rainfall will probably be enough to keep the plants watered. Thin out your plants as they start to crowd each other. Make sure the ground is wet before you start removing lettuces from the row and remember to eat the ones you pull up.

Care and maintenance

Although winter lettuce is bred for cold weather, a sharp drop in temperature may kill off seedlings and young plants. Keep an eye on the weather and protect them with a cloche or similar cover overnight. It should be removed during the day when the temperature has risen.

If you have to leave the cover over your lettuce plants for any length of time, make sure you remove it temporarily every day or so and tend to your plants. The soil under plastic can become mouldy and needs to be agitated from time to time to ensure the lettuce roots don't start to rot. Plants may also need watering and any weeds should be removed with a hoe.

If you are expecting a severe winter, try growing a few winter lettuce in a cold frame or an unheated greenhouse. Don't forget to water plants if you use a greenhouse or cold frame.

Harvesting

Winter lettuce crops can be used as and when the plants are big enough. Varieties that produce a firm head are best left to fully mature, although a leaf or two could be taken from time to time. The cut-and-come-again varieties can and should be picked regularly. The plants will produce more leaves if you use them. Chinese leaf varieties should be left to grow until full maturity – if you can resist! Always check on the manufacturer's growing recommendations for any extra tips on growing and harvesting your chosen variety.

Storing

Winter lettuce is designed to grow throughout the winter months in relatively temperate climates so should be used fresh straight from the garden. It will keep for a day or two in the salad compartment of the fridge if necessary. Don't wash the lettuce before storing. It will last a little longer if kept dry. Close-leaved types of lettuce, like Chinese leaf varieties will store for longer in the fridge but still try to use these fresh from the garden whenever possible

Vitamins

Fresh green vegetables from your garden have all the minerals and enzymes packed into their leaves and a daily portion will help boost the immune system and ward off colds and flu. Lettuces, in particular, are good sources of vitamins A and C and folate. They are a very low-calorie food, making it easier to keep to a calorie-controlled diet even in the winter months.

In ancient times lettuce was used in medicinal preparations. It has mild sedative properties and was eaten in Roman times after meals to induce sleep.

Recipe ideas

We tend to think of lettuce as a summer vegetable and the main ingredient in lovely salads throughout the summer months. But the more robust winter lettuces can also bring a touch of summertime to those dark winter evenings. You can serve virtually any dish with a side salad but cooked lettuce is also a delicious option. Not only will you be providing extra vitamins and minerals for your family, but also crisp textures, colour and, of course, extra taste to your meal.

Lamb and lettuce pan fry

Because winter lettuce is slightly coarser than summer varieties, it is ideal to add to stir fries and pan fries.
● To make this tasty pan fry, heat a little butter and add 4 lamb neck fillets (or similar), cut into chunks. Cook for 6–7 minutes until browned on all sides, then add 2 handfuls of fresh or frozen peas.
● Pour over 150 ml (5 fl oz) chicken stock and simmer for a few minutes until the meat is cooked through.
● Add 3 good handfuls of chopped winter lettuce to the pan and simmer until it just starts to wilt but the colour is still vibrant. Serve straight away with boiled and buttered potatoes.

Salads

Anything that you would normally put into a summer salad can be mixed into the winter salad bowl. You can experiment with different combinations of vegetables according to what you have available. Shred lettuce leaves and put into a salad bowl or serving dish with any or all of the following:
● Green peppers, cut into sticks. Cut a few thin slices in circles across the whole pepper to use as a garnish.
● Finely sliced or chopped onion. Red onions can be slightly milder than white.
● Cherry tomatoes cut in halves or quarters, or sliced larger tomatoes.

● A handful of mixed seeds – pumpkin or sunflower.
● Halved walnuts, pine kernels or other preferred nuts.
● Thinly sliced or grated raw carrots.

Other ideas
● Use in sandwiches and packed lunches – steal a couple of leaves or remember to use the cut-and-come-again varieties.
● Make a healthy and tasty lettuce soup.
● Use lettuce leaves to line a bowl, then spoon a potato salad in the centre. The leaves make the dish look attractive – especially important in winter. Pile on a colourful beetroot, rice or quinoa salad with herbs if you prefer.

Herbs

Herbs have been grown for medicinal, culinary and cosmetic purposes for thousands of years. Many herbs are perennial, which means you can plant them and enjoy them for several years before the plant may need replacing. Rosemary, for example, will live for up to 15 years with a little care and attention along the way.

Using herbs in medicinal preparations should really only be done with expert advice if you've never done it before. However, there are many infusions you can make with herbs that will help prevent colds and flu and also gently treat minor digestive disorders.

Herbs are a great addition to the vegetable patch as their strong scents help deter pests from your plants at the same time as attracting useful bees to your garden, especially when the herbs start flowering. Most will grow pretty much anywhere – in containers on a patio or in a sunny spot, and many will thrive on a bright windowsill. If you have the space, a herb garden is one of the easiest to maintain themed gardens; as well as being fragrant and beautiful to look at, it is also useful. Remember to use your herbs as they like to be picked regularly.

Sage

Sage, as its common name suggests, was considered the herb of wisdom in ancient times and was believed to bestow immortality. It has been used for centuries in medicinal preparations for various ailments and, although these days it tends to be used more frequently in the kitchen, recent studies have shown that a glass of sage tea every day can help reduce menopausal symptoms.

Whether used as a medicinal or culinary herb, sage takes very little looking after and is a perfect addition to a herb garden, and the variegated leaf varieties will brighten up your garden even more.

Propagation

Seed

Growing sage from seed requires a little patience as the plants should be left to grow for a year before using them. If you choose to try your hand at sowing seed, prepare well-drained trays or pots of fresh compost and sow seed in early spring. Keep pots inside or in a greenhouse and water regularly but don't over-water. Sage is native to the Mediterranean so isn't a thirsty plant and copes well in moderate heat. In the early stages of growth it needs warmth. Plant outside later in the year after all danger of frost has passed.

Layering

Because sage is a woody plant, it's fairly simple to propagate new plants from layering the old one. Choose a healthy lower-growing branch from a well-established plant. Spread it on the ground and hold down with a V-shaped peg where it comfortably touches the soil. A smooth stone or small rock can be used instead of a peg. Cover with soil, then water.

This can be done in the autumn and with the right conditions, your new plant may be ready for potting on or replanting in the following spring. Carefully check that the layered branch has produced roots, remove the peg and then cut the stem from the mother plant. Your new plant can be left to grow on or can be transplanted at this point.

Cuttings

Sage can also be propagated from cuttings. Take 7.5–10 cm (3–4 in) cuttings from a healthy plant and push, cut end down, into well-drained pots of fresh compost. Protect from the cold and water regularly, but again don't over-water. When the cuttings have produced roots they can be transplanted. If you don't want to wait for seeds, and you haven't access to a sage plant to take cuttings or layer from, buy a healthy plant from a garden centre or other good garden supplier. If the plants have been grown inside, don't put them outside too early – wait until the danger of frost has passed.

LEFT *Wait until the soil has warmed up and the danger of night frost has passed before planting out young sage plants.*

in a very convenient shape, and never seems to need pruning, but doesn't always produce flowers. Flowering sage benefits from being cut back after the plant has finished flowering. Simply cut the dead wood back. This gives it a chance to rest and produce new growth.

Harvesting

All herbs like to be used. If your plants are started from seed, you should wait a year before picking the leaves. Otherwise, use sage as you need it, as soon as the stems are about 15 cm (6 in) high. Pick leaves from different stems of the plant to allow it to regrow and produce more foliage. Stripping one branch puts pressure on the plant and it may not thrive as it should.

Storing

Sage can often be picked fresh all year round, however it can also be dried or frozen if you expect a cold winter. To dry, hang sprigs of sage upside down in paper bags so they don't get dusty. When the leaves are completely dry, crumble into a jar and label. To freeze, strip the leaves from the stem and freeze quickly.

Vitamins

Sage contains significant amounts of vitamin C, calcium and iron. It is an effective herb for reducing night sweats and other medical conditions. Its volatile oils are transformed into helpful medicinal aids, but the oils contain toxins so should not be taken in large doses. Years ago, sage was used to treat memory loss and digestive disorders.

Planting out

When the temperature of the soil has warmed up and the risk of frost has passed, put young sage plants outside, allowing enough space between them. Transplant into large containers or pots if you prefer and keep in a fairly sunny spot. The most important element for sage to thrive is well-drained soil. Never let the ground become waterlogged. Sage does not cope well in very cold spells so bring indoors if you are facing a very severe winter. However, I have had sage tolerate 15 cm (6 in) of snow with no problems.

Care and maintenance

You may find your sage plants die back in the winter. Mulch the soil with grass clippings or similar organic material and remove early in the spring to allow the plant to start growing again. Sage plants will live happily for many years, although they can get straggly after four or five years. Cut back your plants to shape them and take a few cuttings or layer in a few more plants to keep your supply going. Different varieties will have different needs. Some variegated sage grows

Recipe ideas

Sage is a strong-tasting herb and should be added to food in moderation. Too much can be overpowering and can make the rest of the dish taste bitter. However, it complements chicken and other poultry beautifully and sage stuffing is probably one of the most well-known chicken accompaniments.

Sage tea

An infusion of sage is not only a nutritious drink, it will also aid digestion and help with various minor ailments. Simply pick a few healthy leaves and put into a jug. Then pour over boiling water and cover the jug. Leave to infuse for 5–10 minutes and strain into a glass or small cup. Drink while still warm.

Sage and onion stuffing

Sage and onion stuffing has been available in packet form for many years, but it's always extra tasty if made from scratch at home.

- Peel 4 medium-sized onions. Make sure they are crisp and have no damaged or softened parts. Put them into a pan and cover with water. Bring to the boil, then reduce the heat and simmer for about ten minutes, or until the onions are cooked.
- In the last couple of minutes of cooking time, add ten sage leaves to the pan. Drain well and leave to cool for a few minutes.
- Chop onions and sage very finely in a large bowl. Stir in about 150 g (5 oz) breadcrumbs and 50 g (2 oz) softened butter. Mix together well and bind with an egg yolk. Add salt and pepper to taste. Shape into balls to make individual portions and bake on a baking sheet for 20 minutes or until slightly crisp.

Butternut squash and sage risotto

Squash and sage together is a really tasty combination. This risotto has an autumnal feel, but is a great veggie supper at any time.

- Peel and cut a butternut squash into bite-sized chunks, toss in olive oil, add a handful of finely chopped sage and roast in the oven for 30 minutes.
- While the squash is roasting, prepare the risotto. Make up 1.5 litres (3 pt) vegetable stock, bring it to the boil and keep it on a low simmer.
- In a separate pan, melt a knob of butter and sweat a finely chopped onion for 8–10 minutes until soft and translucent.
- Add 300 g (12 oz) Arborio rice and stir continuously for a couple of minutes until the edges of the grain become transparent.
- Pour in a small glass of white wine and simmer until evaporated. Add the stock, a ladleful at a time and stir continuously until all the stock has been absorbed. After 25–30 minutes the risotto will turn creamy, at which point it should be taken off the heat.
- Fry a small handful of whole sage leaves in a little olive oil, then drain on absorbent kitchen paper.
- When the squash is cooked, mash half of it into a purée and leave half as chunks. Stir the purée into the risotto along with a handful of grated Parmesan. Serve scattered with the chunks of squash and the crispy sage leaves.

Other ideas

Because sage complements roast chicken so well, consider adding it to other poultry dishes.

- Add left-over cooked chicken to stir-fry vegetables in a large pan or wok, and stir into the pan a few very finely chopped sage leaves very finely . Always make sure that reheated meat is piping hot right through before serving.
- Add a chopped sage leaf or two to chicken burgers or rissoles to give that Sunday-roast taste to a midweek leftover meal!
- Add 2 or 3 whole sage leaves to the roasting tin when cooking any poultry, pieces or whole birds.
- Butter-fried sage leaves are a perfect companion to pumpkin ravioli.

Rosemary

All herbs have legends about magical qualities attached to them, and rosemary is no exception. Rosemary appears in records over thousands of years and was widely believed to improve the memory. Modern studies have shown that rosemary does, in fact, have an effect on the brain, so there may be reason to believe that ancient people knew what they were talking about!

Traditionally, rosemary is burned at weddings and funerals. It is a herb associated with love and is included in a bride's bouquet for luck. Mourners at a funeral throw a sprig into the grave, bestowing loving memories of the deceased.

Propagation

Seed

Rosemary is not an easy herb to propagate from seed, but it can be done. Buy seed from a good supplier and check on the manufacturer's sowing recommendations before you start. Generally seed should be sown in well-drained pots or trays of fresh compost early in spring and kept indoors until later in the year. Alternatively, seed can be sown directly outside after all danger of frost has passed. Choose a well-drained sunny spot in the garden. Sow seed in shallow drills and remove weaker plants when the seedlings are a few centimetres high. Leave to grow on and transplant if necessary the following year or when the plants are growing well and have developed a good root system.

Layering

As with sage and many other herbs, rosemary is a woody plant and propagates successfully by layering. Choose a well-established healthy plant and layer the lowest branch or branches along the ground. Secure the branch with a V-shaped peg and cover with a very light sandy soil, then water. A smooth stone or small rock can be used instead of a peg. A new plant should grow from the stem and will, in the right conditions, develop roots. Cut from the 'mother' plant when the new plant is growing well and has developed its own root system. Then either leave to grow where it is or transplant if necessary. Rosemary also does well in a pot so consider moving your new plant to a container.

Cuttings

Take several 7.5–10 cm (3–4 in) cuttings from a healthy, well-established plant after it has finished flowering for the year. Push the cuttings – cut end down – into a well-drained pot of fresh compost and then water it well. The soil should not be left to dry out completely but also should not be over-watered. Look after your cuttings until they have started to grow and develop roots; once they have you can pot them on or plant outside if necessary.

LEFT *Increase rosemary by take cuttings and placing in a pot of well-drained compost, but don't overdo the watering.*

Harvesting

Pick rosemary as you need it. Cut sprigs from healthy plants and try not to take too many stems from a plant at one time unless it is a well-established specimen. Cut 15–20 cm (6–8 in) stems, then remove the leaves by running your fingers or a knife along the stems. Plants grown from seed should be left to develop for the first couple of years or so.

Storing

In most climates rosemary will stay evergreen throughout the year and can be picked fresh when needed. However, if a very harsh winter is expected, leaves can be dried. Hang in an airy place until completely dry. You can use paper bags to prevent needles dropping to the floor. Store in a jar out of direct light. Dried leaves can be crumbled easily and added to meals through the winter. Sprigs can also be frozen, although, because they are often evergreen and also dry successfully, freezing seems unnecessary.

Vitamins

Rich in iron, calcium and vitamin B6, rosemary is a useful herb, and although it isn't widely used in medicinal preparations these days, it can be employed in a number of ways. Add rosemary to the bath to relieve tension – make a small muslin bag and fill with rosemary leaves, then hang from the running tap. Or put a sprig under your pillow to encourage a good night's sleep. The essential oil extracted from rosemary is used widely in the cosmetic industry.

Planting out

Rosemary is originally a Mediterranean plant, so thrives in well-drained soil; it should never be allowed to become waterlogged. Shrubs tend to grow well near a wall or rockery and you should choose a sunny spot for them in your garden or grow in large containers on a bright patio. A healthy plant can live for up to 20 years so choose your spot well – it's far better not to move a larger plant later on.

Fully established, they can grow up to about 1.2 m (4 ft) high, so should be positioned near the back of a herb garden in order to avoid shading lower-growing plants. Rosemary is an evergreen plant and is a bright and colourful herb to include in the garden. If you can afford the space, plant a rosemary shrub on a corner of your vegetable patch.

Care and maintenance

If the winter is expected to be very cold, keep new cuttings indoors in a greenhouse or conservatory, or in a sheltered spot until the weather warms up a little. Although rosemary is a hardy shrub once established outside, it will appreciate a little care and attention during the first year while it is getting established.

Recipe ideas

Rosemary complements many dishes and has traditionally been used with pork, fish and poultry. In recent years, rosemary has also been a popular addition to lamb recipes.

Salads

The texture of the leaves doesn't lend itself well to salads particularly, although well-chopped or crumbled dried leaves can be stirred into a green salad. More often, rosemary is used to flavour oils and vinegars, which are in turn used to dress salads. Simply choose a healthy sprig or two from a well-established plant and put into a bottle of white wine vinegar or olive oil. Seal the bottle and leave in a cool dark place for a couple of weeks to infuse.

Meat dishes

● A sprig or two placed between the leg and breast of a chicken or turkey will help flavour the meat. Or strip the leaves from the stems and sprinkle the leaves into the cooking oil in the bottom of a roasting dish before adding the meat and/or vegetables. You can also add rosemary to stews, casseroles and other one-pot meals.

● Bouquet garni is a popular addition to stews and casseroles and as there isn't any defined recipe, you can make your own from the herbs you prefer and have available. Rosemary, bay leaves, parsley and thyme are all good herbs to add to the bunch. Simply collect a few and tie together with string and add to the pot. Remember to remove before serving.

Red onion and rosemary focaccia

Focaccia is the perfect accompaniment to many Italian dishes and makes an excellent bread for dipping in sauces and olive oils.

● To make the dough, tip 500 g (1 lb) strong white bread flour, 7 g (1 packet) dried yeast and a pinch of salt into a large bowl. Make a well in the centre and pour in most of 350 ml (12 fl oz) lukewarm water, then use your fingers to combine the flour and water until you make a pillowy, workable dough, adding a splash more water as necessary.

● Knead the dough on a lightly floured surface for at least 10 minutes until smooth and elastic. Place in a bowl and cover with cling film and leave to rise in a warm place until it has risen to double the size.

● When it has risen, knock back and stretch it to fill a swiss roll tin. Leave the dough to prove for 20 minutes. Preheat the oven to 200°C (400°F/gas mark 6).

● Meanwhile, slice 2 large red onions and gather a handful of rosemary sprigs, stripping the leaves from the branches. Spread the onions over the dough and scatter over the rosemary leaves. Press dimples into the dough with your fingers and drizzle over a generous amount of olive oil and a pinch of sea salt.

● Bake for 30 minutes until golden. When cool, cut or tear into pieces for a more rustic look.

Other ideas

Rosemary can be added to almost any dish you choose, depending on the tastes of the individual. It also has some functional uses around the kitchen and when eating alfresco.

● Add a tablespoon or two of chopped leaves to apples when making apple jam or jellies.

● Use the stems as skewers. Strip the leaves and thread cubes of meat and vegetables onto the stems before barbecuing or grilling. The rosemary oil in the stem will add flavour to the meat and veg.

● Sprinkle a few leaves or a whole sprig on the barbecue coals to keep the mosquitoes and midges away on a summer night.

● Put chopped rosemary leaves into the roasting tin along with olive oil when making roast potatoes.

Thyme

Thyme has been used as a medicinal herb since ancient times. Roman soldiers were encouraged to bathe in thyme before going into battle as it was believed to bestow courage, and the ancient Greeks used thyme for embalming. Thyme leaves were also embroidered onto cherished linen and given as gifts to acknowledge bravery or adoration. As well as being used to flavour foods, thyme was often employed as a meat preservative. These days, thyme is grown for culinary and medicinal purposes – it soothes sore throats and eases cold and flu symptoms. Native to the Mediterranean, thyme prefers a light dry soil and will thrive on walls and very well-drained soil.

Propagation

Seed

Thyme can be started from seed quite easily but should be left to grow and become established for a year or so before you begin taking its leaves. If you have the patience, it is certainly worth having a go at propagating from seed. Seed can be sown indoors in well-drained trays or pots of fresh compost and kept warm and watered until later in the year. Transplant outside after all danger of frost has passed.

You can also sow the seeds outside. To do so, place the seeds in shallow drills in late spring, again after all danger of frost has passed. Check on your seed packet for the manufacturer's growing advice before you start, as different varieties will have different requirements. Thyme grows successfully in pots and containers, and won't mind a little drying out from time to time. It will need some water though, so don't forget about your thyme entirely.

Root division

Thyme is a woody shrub and will benefit from being divided into smaller clumps every few years. Either later in the year after the plant has finished flowering, or very early before it starts to grow in the spring are probably the best times. Try to avoid disturbing your plants when the ground is very cold, though. Dig carefully around your plant and divide into two or more pieces. Gently but firmly pull the clump of roots apart, then replant immediately so the roots are not exposed for too long. Water well after transplanting and cover with a cloche or similar protection after planting if the winter is particularly harsh.

Cuttings

Start new plants by taking cuttings from a healthy and well-established plant. Cut 7.5–10 cm (3–4 in) pieces of stem with a sharp knife or secateurs. Push, cut end down, into well-drained pots of fresh compost and water gently. Keep soil damp but not too wet. Keep

pots of cuttings indoors or in a greenhouse until they have developed roots and are starting to grow. They should be planted outside in early summer, when the ground has warmed up a little.

Planting out

Thyme likes a light soil in a sunny spot and will thrive near walls, rockeries or in raised beds. It is possible to grow in heavier soil, but it loses some of its strength of taste and smell. Thyme is also a very suitable container herb, especially as it doesn't mind if you forget to water it for a while. Plant in a container on the patio or any sunny spot in your garden. It will also do well in pots or containers indoors as long as it has enough light.

Care and maintenance

Thyme must never be allowed to become waterlogged. In fact, it will survive longer without any water than with too much, so never be tempted to over-water. Generally, thyme will stay green throughout the winter months making it an ideal winter herb to grow. If your plant does die back or the temperature is very low, a mulch around the roots will help to protect it. Remember to remove the mulch before the following spring if the mulch hasn't decomposed to allow the plant to grow.

Harvesting

Leave any plants you have propagated from seed to grow for the first year so that they develop a strong root structure. After that, or with older plants, pick sprigs as and when required. As with most herbs, thyme likes to be picked regularly and will produce more foliage if you use it. After flowering, plant growth tends to slow down for the year. If you are expecting a very cold winter and have young thyme plants, collect some leaves to dry or freeze – just in case.

Storing

Thyme will often stay green throughout the year and should be picked fresh wherever possible for the full benefits of taste and nutrition. However, it can also be successfully dried or frozen. To dry, either lay stems or separate leaves out on a tray in a dry place until dry enough to crumble. Or stems can be hung in paper bags in a cool airy place until dry. Crumble leaves into a jar, label and store out of direct light. If you prefer to freeze them, lay stems on a freezer tray and freeze quickly. Put leaves in a suitable container and label, before storing in the freezer.

Vitamins

A good source of iron, thyme is also a wonderful healing herb. It has natural antiseptic properties and is also a quick remedy for cuts and grazes in the garden. The natural oil, thymol, is considered to be a valuable ingredient in many commercial medications.

Recipe ideas

Thyme is a useful herb to have in the kitchen and enhances the taste of many fish and meat dishes. It is popular in many countries and a sprig of thyme is often included in bouquet garni (a bunch of fresh herbs added to soups and stews during cooking and removed before serving). Thyme is also one of the ingredients of *herbes de provence* – a mixture of herbs often available in dried form, but is much tastier when fresh. Many recipes measure thyme by the tablespoon. In these cases, remove leaves from the stem first.

Thyme tea

To soothe cold and flu symptoms, put a handful of thyme leaves in a jug and pour over boiling water. Cover and leave to stand for five minutes, then strain into a glass or cup and add a dash of lemon juice and a teaspoon of clear honey. Sip while still warm.

Easy tomato and thyme cod

When you would rather be on the sofa than in the kitchen, this quick supper couldn't be simpler. Heat a little oil in a pan and fry a finely chopped onion until soft. Stir in a 400 g (14 oz) can chopped tomatoes, 1 tsp brown sugar, a small handful of thyme leaves and a good splash of soy sauce. Bring to the boil, then simmer for 5 minutes. Gently place the cod into the sauce, cover and simmer gently for 8–10 minutes until the fish is cooked. Serve with potatoes or crusty bread.

Try lemon and thyme together…

• Add a sprig of thyme to the lemonade jug or other lemon-based drink.
• For a taste of summer, stir a few fresh leaves into the salad bowl with a squeeze of lemon or make a dressing adding finely chopped fresh leaves.
• Add thyme leaves to a chicken stir fry early in the cooking time. Stir in a little freshly squeezed lemon juice just before serving.

ABOVE *Thyme can be planted out in open ground but is also equally happy in pots and containers.*

Other ideas

• Add whole sprigs to the cooking tin when roasting a joint of meat or vegetables. Or remove the leaves from the stems and sprinkle into the bottom of the pan. Thyme releases its flavours slowly and should be added, in most cases, early on in the cooking time.
• Sprinkle a few leaves onto halved tomatoes before 'sun-drying' them in the oven. Arrange tomatoes on a baking tray and sprinkle with thyme. Set oven at lowest temperature and remove tomatoes once they are dry. Leave the oven door ajar if the tomatoes start to 'cook'. Cool completely then store the tomatoes in containers until required.
• Try stirring some tiny thyme leaves (chop if necessary) into soft cheese before spreading on sandwiches or mixing with warm pasta.

Garlic

No good cook should be without onions or garlic, and luckily garlic is fairly straightforward to grow. It stores well for most of the winter months and adds depth of flavour to hearty winter soups, stews and casserole dishes.

Garlic is steeped in legend and myth, including the idea that it can ward off evil spirits. In fact, its strong scent will deter most pests from your garden and will indeed protect your crops. Garlic's antiseptic qualities may also help ward off viruses and diseases in humans too!

Seed

Garlic seeds are simply the cloves from the garlic bulb. It is possible to grow further bulbs from cloves that have been taken from supermarket-bought garlic; however, for the best crops, buy hybrid bulbs from a reputable garden supplier as these have been bred specially for growing at home. If you do decide to have a go at growing from a supermarket bulb rather than a hybrid, at least make sure that the garlic has been grown organically.

There are many different hybrid varieties of garlic available, from Red Sicilian to Elephant garlic, mostly originating from France. Some are suitable for autumn planting and you should check on the manufacturer's growing recommendations before you buy these. Autumn-planted bulbs may need a little protection during the colder months of the year.

If you have the space available, try a couple of different varieties of garlic so you know what grows best in your garden for the following year.

Planting out

Garlic is a hardy plant and will tolerate low temperatures. It can be planted out early in the year, although some varieties can also be planted in autumn. For spring sowings, dig over the ground during the previous autumn if you can or as soon as the soil is workable in early spring. Clear any perennial weeds and large stones.

It's important to remember not to over-fertilize the soil when growing garlic. Over-feeding will encourage the plant to develop more leaf and it won't put so much energy into producing the desirable swollen garlic bulb. Make sure the soil is well drained and rake the ground over to a fairly fine consistency. Plant the garlic cloves about 20 cm (8 in) apart, leaving 30 cm (12 in) or more between rows so that you have enough room to maintain and weed your plants. Plant the base end down and leave the tip of each clove just showing above the ground.

Garlic is also suitable for container growing as each

plant takes up little space and doesn't need a great depth of soil. Don't forget to water them though. The soil in containers and pots dries out quickly and garlic won't thrive if it doesn't get enough water, but again make sure the pots are well drained and in no danger of being waterlogged.

Care and maintenance

If you find that birds are a problem, you may want to cover the tips of the cloves lightly with soil or put a protective wildlife-friendly net over them until they put down roots. Once established, the cloves won't pull out of the ground easily. Also remember to water gently after planting. Garlic is generally sown in early spring so should get enough rain water, but keep an eye on the soil as it should not be allowed to dry out. Pull out any stray weeds to give your plants lots of space to develop.

Garlic is a hardy plant and because of its strong scent it does not tend to attract predators. The only thing that can be a problem with garlic is 'bolting' or running to seed too quickly. Many plants bolt in hot dry weather, which you can discourage by shading them a little if the days are long and hot. Water regularly if there isn't sufficient rainfall to keep the soil damp. If your garlic plants do run to seed – when they send out a hard stem from the middle of the bulb – fold over the leaves or snap the hard woody stem off. These bulbs won't store as well as the others, so should be used first.

Harvesting

Garlic behaves in the same way as onions and shallots. It will grow until the bulb is developed to its full size then the leaves start to droop and dry out. Some growers fold the leaves down when they start to dry,

while others just leave them. If you feel like tidying up the vegetable patch, simply fold the leaves over and then leave them to die back completely.

Before the weather changes in the autumn, all garlic should be lifted. Gently loosen the soil around each bulb if necessary and pull out of the ground. Lay on dry earth or trays for an hour or two to dry out, before brushing off any excess soil and storing.

Storing

The best way to store garlic is in plaits if you can. It's not only practical but also decorates the kitchen nicely. Simply plait the leaves together when they are dry but not crumbly. This take a little practice but is well worth the effort. If plaiting isn't the best option for you, remove leaves by cutting them about a centimetre or so above the bulb, and store in single layers in cardboard boxes or wooden trays. Keep out of direct light in a cool dry place.

Vitamins

Rich in vitamins B and C and minerals calcium and iron, garlic also has antibacterial, antiviral and antifungal properties. It is an excellent addition to the diet in the winter months as it will help ward off colds and flu viruses. The Romans believed it to be a herb of strength and soldiers were encouraged to eat it daily. It is also said that garlic will cleanse the blood, which could, of course, be the basis of the myths about warding off evil spirits. Garlic should be consumed in smaller doses by those suffering with eczema or other skin complaints, as it can irritate the condition.

Recipe ideas

Along with onions, no good chef would be without a clove or two of garlic in the kitchen. And less-than-perfect cooks will be able to hide all sorts of culinary hiccups with a crushed clove in the recipe! Garlic is used in cuisines around the world, from Chinese to French and Mediterranean to Russian.

Garlic bread

This goes with so many family dishes – spaghetti bolognaise, chilli, soups or salads. Use a long French loaf or small baguettes – this is an excellent way to use up French bread that is a day older than it should be.
- Using a sharp knife or a bread knife, cut slits along the loaf, not quite cutting right through so that it stays together. Make slits every couple of centimetres or so.
- Blend a couple of cloves of garlic with slightly softened butter or a butter substitute, and stir in some finely chopped fresh parsley. Using a knife, divide the garlic and herb butter between the slices. Any leftover butter can be spread lightly over the top of the loaf.
- Wrap the loaf in foil and put on a baking sheet. Pop into a preheated medium oven for about 20 minutes or until hot right through. Unwrap and serve hot.

Stuffed garlic mushrooms

These make a great starter or a tasty light lunch.
- In a pan, fry 2 finely chopped shallots and 2 garlic cloves until soft.
- Mix with 250 g (9 oz) breadcrumbs, a little chopped parsley if available and a pinch of salt and pepper.
- Wash and stem around 12 large mushrooms and place in a greased ovenproof dish.
- Pack the breadcrumb mixture into each mushroom cap and top each one with grated mozzarella cheese.
- Bake in a medium oven for 10–15 or until the cheese is melted and golden and the mushrooms are cooked right through.

Other ideas

- Toss drained cooked carrots in finely chopped garlic and a knob of butter before serving.
- To give just a hint of garlic to a salad, rub a halved clove of garlic around the inside of the bowl before filling with salad ingredients.
- Or for more of a garlic kick, finely chop a clove or two and add it to your salad dressing.
- Rub a half clove of garlic on toasted French bread, then drizzle with olive oil to make delicious bruschetta. Top with tomatoes for a real treat.

Chives

Chives are part of the same family of plants as onions, shallots and garlic. They have similar properties to onions but are milder in taste and are a useful herb to grow in the kitchen garden, in containers or even on the kitchen windowsill. They will keep fresh and green all year round on a sunny windowsill as long as you remember to water them occasionally. Chives are also useful if planted in the garden near vegetables to help deter pests. Chives are a fairly hardy perennial plant, which means that one plant should last many years given the right conditions.

Propagation

Seed

There are different chive seeds available including a 'garlic' variety – these are sometimes called Chinese chives. Some varieties produce a white flower and others purple so grow a few of each to enhance your herb garden with the different coloured blooms. Chive flowers, as well as the leaves, are edible.

Chives are one of the few plants in the onion family that will grow easily from seed. The germination rate is usually fairly quick, so chives are great plants for beginners, especially children, who quite like to see rapid results. There are pots on the market that are specially designed for children to grow chives as 'hair' over a smiley-faced pot. Alternatively, start seed off in early spring by sowing thinly in well-drained trays or pots of fresh compost. Check the sowing recommendations on your seed packet for regional variations before you start.

Keep your chive seed warm and watered but obviously don't over-water either until the seeds have germinated. Don't let the seedlings dry out.

Root division

Dig up a healthy chive plant that has been established for a year or two. To avoid damaging the roots, dig carefully around the plant when the ground is wet, then gently but firmly separate the roots into two or more clumps and replant immediately. Water well immediately after planting.

Planting out

After all danger of frost has passed, chives can be planted out in the garden. As long as the ground is well drained and in a reasonably sunny spot, chive plants can be positioned around the garden. They make good border plants as they don't grow very tall and are

attractive to look at. Plant one or two chives on the corners of your vegetable plot to help deter bugs and attract bees.

Handle the seedlings carefully, and allow space for them to grow. Although they like a sunny spot, chives may suffer if exposed to long hot dry periods. Make sure they get enough water, and rig up a little shade for them if the weather is scorching.

Care and maintenance

Chives are a fairly hardy plant and will thrive in less-than-perfect soil. However, if the soil is very poor they will benefit from an organic feed from time to time. Chives are rarely affected by bugs and viruses, but to keep them healthy and producing fresh green foliage every year, they should be separated by root division every few years. There are no hard and fast rules as to how often they should be divided. The best thing is to check each plant for any signs of rotting in the centre or if they are simply getting too big for their allocated space. In a very cold winter, plants may die back but should revive in the spring. In a severe winter, mulch will protect the roots, but remember to remove any undecomposed matter before spring.

Harvesting

With a little luck and attention, a chive plant will produce fresh green leaves practically all year round. Always use sharp scissors and cut leaves from the outside of the plant. Cutting from the middle restricts the cut leaves from growing again as they have less light. The outside leaves regrow easily. Cut to about 5–7.5 cm (2–3 in) from the ground, depending on the size of your plant. Flowers can be collected as soon as they appear – cut down the flower stalks when removing the flowers. After the plant has finished flowering, cut down the whole plant to 5–7.5 cm (2–3 in) high and it will start producing leaves again. Plants grown from seed should be used when they are growing well and have many leaves.

Storing

As chives will stay evergreen most of the year it is unlikely you will need to store them. However, if the winters are severe in your area, fresh chives can be frozen quickly and stored for several months. Either lay on trays and freeze quickly then put into a suitable container and label. Or cut into small pieces and put into ice cube trays before filling with water and freezing. Simply defrost ice cubes to retrieve the chives.

Vitamins

Chives have similar properties to the other members of the onion family, although the overall constituents tend to be weaker than onions or garlic. They are a useful herb to grow in the kitchen garden, but will also aid in alleviating colds and flu symptoms as do other members of the onion family. Chives are also considered to be an effective digestive aid. They have significant amounts of vitamin C, calcium and iron with hardly any calories or fat.

Recipe ideas

Chives can brighten up any dish with a hint of onion flavour. They are perfect to add to dishes for those who aren't keen on the stronger-tasting onion or shallot.

Salads

Snip chives into small pieces with scissors or chop with a sharp knife. Stir into the salad bowl for just a hint of onion flavour. Chives will pep up any plain green salad and are extremely good snipped over a ripe tomato salad dressed with olive oil and lemon.

Potato salad

Chives bring out the taste of potatoes like no other herb and you can use them snipped over plain boiled new potatoes or in a potato salad.
- Peel and wash potatoes, then cut into cubes. Put into a pan and cover with water. Bring to the boil, then reduce heat and simmer until potatoes are just cooked. Don't let them get too soft. Drain well and leave to cool completely.
- Make a dressing with half mayonnaise and half natural yoghurt, or any other combination you prefer. Crème fraîche can be used instead of mayonnaise or yoghurt. A little cream could be added if calories aren't an issue.
- Stir chopped chives to taste into the dressing.
- When the potatoes are completely cold put into a serving dish and gently stir in the dressing.
- Chill in the fridge for 10 minutes or so before serving. A few chopped chives can be sprinkled over the top of the dish to garnish.

Other ideas

- Sprinkle chopped fresh chives over cheese on toast and then pop under the grill for a minute or two.
- Add finely chopped chives to scrambled egg, omelettes or quiche mixtures before cooking.
- Add fresh chives cut into small pieces to sandwiches.

- Chives are particularly good with tuna or egg mayonnaise sandwiches.
- Mix some chives with sour cream and use to top a piping hot jacket potato.
- Nibble a few chives if you are hanging around in the kitchen rather than diving into the biscuit tin. They take the edge off your hunger and prepare your taste buds for savoury food rather than sweet tastes.

Parsley

Parsley is probably one of the most popular and common herbs, although for many years its role as a garnish meant that it often stayed on the plate rather than being eaten. Recent studies have shown that parsley is one of the most nutritious herbs we can grow – packed with vitamins, it is an excellent herb to add to many dishes. Parsley's breath-freshening qualities also make it an ideal herb to serve with garlic dishes.

Originating in the Mediterranean region, parsley is widely cultivated throughout the world. It is a biennial plant so produces leaves in the first year and flowers and seed in its second year of growth.

Seed

There are a number of parsley varieties that will grow readily in the kitchen garden. The most popular are the curly-leafed variety (often used as a garnish) and a flat-leafed Italian variety. Both are equally tasty and nutritious. Sow parsley every year for a constant supply but leave the plants in the ground if you can. Seed can take up to six weeks to germinate and pots and trays will need to be kept warm and watered regularly. Some growers soak seed in water for a few hours before sowing to speed up the process.

In early spring, prepare well-drained pots of fresh compost and sow a few seeds in each. Check the manufacturer's growing recommendations for regional variations. Keep pots in a warm bright place and well watered; although they must never become waterlogged, the soil should always be damp or the seeds won't germinate. When the seedlings are a few centimetres high, remove weaker ones from the pots and leave the strongest plant in each pot to grow on.

In some areas parsley can be sown directly outside, although unless you have a long growing season, you may find the plants don't develop as well as those started earlier in a greenhouse. If you do decide to sow seed outside, wait until all danger of frost has passed and sow thinly in shallow drills. Remove weaker plants when the seedlings are a few centimetres high to give the others space to grow.

Planting out

Parsley is a very nutritious herb, but draws its minerals and vitamins from the soil; it is therefore a heavy-feeding plant so won't grow well in poor soil. Choose a sunny well-drained spot in the garden. Dig in plenty of compost or well-rotted manure a month or two before growing if necessary. Dig over the ground, removing any perennial weeds, non-organic debris and large stones and rake over to a fine consistency. Before removing plants from their pots, soak well in water to

LEFT *Parsley is a herb that needs good soil in order to thrive, and will benefit from regular feeding.*

strip a plant of all its leaves; take a few from each plant to allow the plants to push up more foliage. When the plant has obviously stopped producing any more leaf, cut a few sprigs for storing.

Leave the plants in the ground to over-winter. If conditions are good, they will produce flowers and then seeds in the following spring, which can be collected for sowing in subsequent years or used in the kitchen to flavour food.

Storing

Parsley will keep for a few days in the salad compartment of the fridge, and like many herbs is best when used fresh. It can also be frozen. Freeze whole stems quickly on a suitable tray, pack in containers or freezer bags and label before putting in the freezer. Parsley also dries successfully. Hang stems in a dark, dry and airy place over card or put into paper bags before hanging in order to collect any falling leaves. When completely dry, crumble into jars and label. Store out of direct light. Dried parsley will keep its taste for many months.

Vitamins

Gram for gram, parsley has more vitamin C than citrus fruits. Logically you would have to eat a huge amount of parsley to get the same amount of vitamin C as you would from an orange, but it is a worthy herb to add to any dish. Parsley is also packed with iron and other vitamins and minerals. It contains significant amounts of calcium and very few calories. Parsley is also very effective at freshening the breath and should be served with all garlic or strong-tasting dishes.

allow the contents of the pot to be removed without damaging the roots. Biodegradable pots can be used if preferred, but the pots should still be soaked in water before planting out. When planting out parsley plants allow plenty of space for them to grow into and check on your seed packet for any spacing recommendations. Water well after planting.

Care and maintenance

Keep the soil around the plants weed-free and water regularly in dry weather. Parsley plants will benefit from an organic feed every week or two, especially if your soil has been used for crops beforehand. Take care plants don't dry out. In very long hot dry periods, they may appreciate a little shade from the midday sun.

Harvesting

You can start using parsley when the plants are about 20 cm (8 in) high. This gives them adequate time to develop their roots. Pick stems as required but don't

Recipe ideas

It's such a shame that parsley is all too often left on the side of the plate or used as a garnish rather than actually being eaten in recipes for extra flavour. By doing this, it could be that we are leaving the most nutritious part of the meal uneaten. Parsley root is also edible and can be scrubbed, sliced and added to casseroles, soups and stews.

Parsley pie

Parsley pie is an old Cornish recipe and is a great way to use up leftovers.

- Half-fill an ovenproof dish with chopped fresh parsley. Then stir in any leftover meat (traditionally lamb) or vegetables.
- Hard-boil a couple of eggs and add them to the dish.
- Pour a vegetable or chicken stock almost up to the level of the parsley mixture.
- Roll out enough ready-made shortcrust pastry to fit the top of your dish. Cover the parsley mixture with the pastry and bake in a preheated medium–hot oven 180°C (350°F/gas mark 4) for about 30 minutes. If preferred put a pastry holder in the middle of the dish before adding ingredients. This will hold the pastry off the rest of the food and keep it drier.
- The pastry can also be glazed with a little milk or beaten egg before baking.
- Serve hot with mashed potatoes or green vegetables. Remember when reheating meat, make sure it is piping hot before serving.

Perfect parsley and chickpea salad

- In a large bowl, combine a 400 g (14 oz) tin of drained chickpeas, a finely sliced red onion and half a chopped cucumber, 100 g (4 oz) crumbled feta cheese and a good bunch of roughly chopped parsley.
- To make the dressing, mix 2 tbsp red wine vinegar with 3 tbsp olive oil and season. Pour over the salad and toss to combine all ingredients.

Other ideas

- Use parsley in stews, one-pot meals and tomato sauces by simply chopping some fresh leaves and adding to the pan.
- Combine chopped parsley with bulgar wheat, spring onions, mint leaves, lemon juice and olive oil to make tabouli, a traditional Middle Eastern salad dish.
- Make a rub for meat or fish by mixing chopped parsley with garlic and lemon zest.
- Add a combination of chopped parsley and mint to any green salad.
- Parsley sauce is a traditional accompaniment to broad beans and boiled ham. It is delicious with any fresh garden vegetables but is particularly tasty with beans and peas. The sauce also provides a great savoury base for a creamy chicken pie.

Garden fruits

There are many fruits that can be grown in the garden, making it a delicious and easy experience to get the five-a-day we know we should be having. Harder fruits, such as apples and pears thrive in cooler climates and many of us will have fond memories of the apple tree at the end of the garden. Nowadays, with varieties grafted onto solid rootstock, we can grow apples and pears in smaller spaces and still produce lots of fresh fruit for the family.

As well as hard fruits, soft fruits such as strawberries, raspberries and blackberries can also be grown in most climates. Traditionally a summer fruit, strawberries now come in varieties that produce fruit early and later in the year. They are also a perfect jam ingredient to bring a touch of summer to the winter months. The more exotic fruits – kiwis, bananas and melons – need a long hot growing season and, unless you are set up with a heated greenhouse, these fruits aren't really suitable to grow in a cooler climate. However, every year seems to bring a new hybrid on the market that will cope with a shorter and cooler growing season, so it's worth keeping a look out for new fruits you may be able to grow in your region.

Apples and Pears

If you only have an average-size garden, you may think that it's not practical to grow apple and pear trees, but you don't need a big garden to grow these wonderful fruits. Grafted trees, available at good garden or tree suppliers, are basically varieties of smaller trees grafted onto a hardier rootstock. This restricts the height of the tree. It is possible to start apple and pear trees from seed, but eventually, without the grafting restriction they will grow to 9 m (30 ft) or more in an ideal environment. Traditionally, crab apple is used as rootstock for apple trees especially where they are indigenous and are hardier and more resistant to disease. The same theory applies to pears.

Choosing your trees

Apples

The choice of apple is really a personal preference and you should buy the tree that produces apples you like to eat. Do some research before you buy if you are not sure. From sweet soft varieties right through to the large hard cooking apples, the choice is huge. If you have the space, try a couple of different varieties. Cox's Orange Pippin is sweet and juicy, Russets are drier and there are many crunchy sweet apple varieties that are also suitable for cooking – you don't have to add as much sugar as you do with cooking apple varieties.

Pollination must also be considered. You may be lucky to find a self-pollinating variety but generally two plants are required to pollinate and produce fruit. Check the manufacturer's recommendations before you buy your tree so you have the right stock to produce good crops. Try and match two different varieties that will pollinate each other. Again look for advice when you buy your tree.

Normally apple trees will be sold as one- or two-year-old plants – it's really up to you what to choose. The two-year-old will produce fruit a year earlier than a one-year-old tree, but otherwise, it really doesn't matter. Once established an apple tree will produce fruit for decades from its third year of growth.

Pears

The choice of pears in a supermarket is usually limited to two or three, but there are, in fact, many different varieties you can grow in the home garden. As with apples, choose the ones you and your family like to eat. Pear trees can produce fruit for more than 60 years, although the hybrid grafted trees may have a shorter lifespan. Conference pears are self-pollinating, but will produce more fruit if pollinated by another variety. Check pollination advice before you buy.

Pear trees are often sold as two- or three-year-old plants. They don't tend to fruit until they are five years old though. As with apples, check the growing advice before you buy so you know what to expect.

Buying checklist

- Consider the potential size of your tree
- Look at planting and pruning instructions
- Check pollination requirements
- Make sure bark and roots are healthy and undamaged before you purchase.

All apples and pears can be bought as 'cordons' that stay very small but crop heavily. These are ideal for a small space and can be grown very successfully against a fence or south-facing wall. Small bush varieties are a good choice for a slightly larger space, and if you have an acre or two, why not go for the full-sized versions!

Planting

Generally apple and pear trees are not particularly fussy about soil, although extreme acid or alkaline soil should be regulated before planting to get the most from your trees. Ideally, the soil should be slightly on the acid side, but only slightly. Fruit trees also prefer a sunny spot to give the fruit a chance to develop fully, but will tolerate a little shade. The larger the tree the more tolerant of shade. Smaller varieties that grow in pots or against a fence will need a sunnier spot, and pear trees tend to need more sun than apples. The ground should be well drained, in an area free from frost pockets or wind tunnels.

The soil doesn't have to be rich either. Trees tend to grow well even in slightly poorer soil, although it's best to check the growing recommendations that come with your tree before planting. If the ground hasn't been fed or worked for a while, a light mix of well-rotted manure or compost will help give the tree a bit of a boost. But don't overdo the feeding; trees that live in very rich soil tend to produce a huge amount of foliage but relatively little fruit.

Fruit trees should be planted from winter to spring, generally speaking. Dig over the ground about a month before planting and then dig a hole about 1.2 m (4 ft) deep and 60 cm (2 ft) wide. Incorporate any compost if you are using it. Work organic matter into the soil you dig out until it is fairly crumbly. Leave to settle. When you plant your tree, depth is very important. Look at the rootstock and decide where the soil line was when it was growing. This is easier to find if you have bought a potted tree. With bare root trees, the soil line isn't always obvious, but if you make sure the 'join' in the trunk – the grafted part between the rootstock and stem (or scion) – is a couple of centimetres above the ground after planting you should be okay. Be sure not to add any more compost at this point. Simply plant your tree in the hole and fill with the soil you previously dug out. Firm down well. Heel around the trunk to make sure it's firmly in the ground. If the tree needs a support structure, push this into the ground when planting the tree so as not to damage the roots later. After planting, water well.

Care and maintenance

During the first few years, make sure your fruit trees don't dry out. When they are more established they tend to find water by themselves. However, in long dry periods, your fruit trees may need watering regularly to produce and develop fruits. Keep weed-free, especially when they are young. In a very cold winter, it is a good idea to mulch around the tree to protect the roots from heavy frosts. Don't mulch too close to the trunk or too high as this can cause rotting or encourage harmful insects and disease to the tree. Remove the mulch from around the tree in the spring.

Pruning is also an important part of fruit tree maintenance. When you plant a one-year-old tree, generally the top part should be cut down straight after planting with a sharp pair of secateurs. Make sure there are about four buds left. From the second year, pruning should be done between December and February while the tree is resting. Prune away the black shoots leaving healthy pink shoots to grow on. The idea with a espalier or cordon type apple tree or a bush pear, is to train them to grow against a fence or other support.

Apple trees should have about four fruiting branches every year but pears are better with about six branches. Once the trees are five years old, they should have established their shape and will need very little attention. However, it's a good idea to check them in the winter months so you can remove any damaged or unruly branches. Always double-check on growing and pruning recommendations for your particular type of tree as each variety has its own special needs.

Harvesting

With larger trees, some fruits will drop naturally early in the growing season, but to get the most from your crops, you should thin them later on as necessary. Look at each cluster and remove any damaged or unhealthy-looking fruit. Also each fruit needs space to develop, so removing fruits to give the others more room is important. It's tempting to leave them all to grow but without the right space and air flow, fruit won't develop properly, and may have trouble producing any fruit at all in the following year. Cordons and some hybrids may not require any thinning but always check on the development of the fruit and remove any you think may be unhealthy or damaged. Damaged fruit will attract wasps and may damage other fruits.

The rule of thumb when harvesting apples is to take a fruit gently in your hand, twist it slightly and if it comes away from the tree easily, it's ready to eat. Otherwise simply try one! Pears are generally harvested before they are completely ripe and then ripened off. They should be kept in an airy place out of direct light, but not necessarily in the dark.

All apples and pears should be harvested before

ABOVE *Use sharp secateurs when pruning fruit trees and check each variety's special pruning needs.*

there is any danger of frost and preferably before the autumn rains set in. If the weather is good and fruits are growing well, leave them on the trees until the very last minute to collect them. Use any windfall fruits as they drop from the trees rather than leaving them to rot on the ground or adding to the compost heap.

LEFT *Apples are ready to pick when you can twist the fruit off the branch with ease.*

It's also possible to dry apples and pears. Fruit should be peeled, cored and cut into rings of about 6 mm (⅛ in) thick. Soak for 5 minutes in a solution of 4.5 litres (8 pt) water to 50 g (2 oz) salt. Drain and spread on a baking tray. Dry in a very slow oven for 6–8 hours, leaving the door open slightly. Cool and store in suitable containers out of direct light. Apple rings can be dried in a home food dryer or on trays in the sun if you have long sunny days later in the year. The old-fashioned way was to hang them over a stove strung onto a string or piece of clean dowelling. Pears can be dried in the same way, although hard pears are better cut in slices and blanched for 10 minutes in water and sugar, rather than soaking in a saline solution. Drain and dry. Fruits don't have to be dried to the 'brittle' stage. The dried fruit we buy is usually about 20 per cent water.

Storing

Hard fruit will keep in a fruit bowl for a few days or a week. Softer fruits should be used within a few days. Fruit is notoriously difficult to keep for any length of time, but harder fruits, such as apples and some of the harder varieties of pears will store well in trays or boxes for several months. Make sure there are no damaged fruits and wrap each one in newspaper or tissue paper before placing them in single layers in a wooden or cardboard tray or box.

Store in a cool dark place and use as required. Too dry an atmosphere will cause fruit to age faster, so a little humidity is needed. Never store windfalls; they should be used immediately. Apples that have fallen to the ground will likely have bruising or other damage. Making fruit up into pies, tarts and preserves will add to the length of time you can store your fruit crops.

Vitamins

The saying 'an apple a day keeps the doctor away' really does have some relevance. Apples are high in dietary fibre, they freshen your breath and clean the teeth, exercise the gums, are low in calories and packed with vitamins and minerals. A couple of apples a day will really make a difference to your health.

The skin of apples and the flesh near the surface contains higher quantities of vitamins than the interior, as well as possessing properties that will help lower cholesterol and fight off certain cancer cells. They truly are worth adding to the daily diet.

Apples and pears belong to the same family of plants, and pears are very similar to apples in their vitamin and mineral make-up. Apples and pears also contain pectin which makes them ideal to use when making jam with soft fruits containing less pectin.

Recipe ideas

There are literally hundreds of recipes for apples, both sweet and savoury. Pies, crumbles, sauces, cakes, preserves and butters are just a few suggestions. Pears are also an ideal fruit for using in sweet and savoury dishes. As they are often picked while still a little hard, pears can be softened by cooking.

Stewed apples

Make a simple purée for a quick dessert or use it to accompany roast pork.

- Peel, core and slice apples thinly. Put into a pan and just cover with water. Bring to the boil, then reduce heat and simmer until soft. Harder varieties will take longer to soften.
- Drain and blend in a food processor or simply mash with a fork. Add a little sugar if too sharp.

Apple pie

- Preheat the oven to 180°C (350°F/gas mark 4) then peel, core and slice a couple of large cooking apples. Put into a pan and add a little water to prevent sticking. Cook over a low heat until soft.
- Drain and put apples into a lightly buttered ovenproof dish. Add a little water and 2–3 tbsp sugar if the apples are sharp. Sprinkle over 1 tsp cinnamon.
- Put a pastry holder or upturned egg cup in the middle of the dish to hold the pastry away from the apples. Using ready-made shortcrust pastry, roll out and lay over the top of the dish.
- Using a fine skewer, make a few air holes in the pastry. Brush with beaten egg or milk and put into the oven for 30–40 minutes depending on the size of your dish. When golden brown remove from the oven.

Apples and cheese

Apples are one of the best fruits to accompany cheese.

- Spear cubes of hard cheese and wedges of apple onto cocktail sticks for a quick snack.

- Grate apple and add to bread and cheese.
- Apple pie and a slice of Cheddar is a wonderful combination – the sweet apple and pastry are an excellent foil for the tang of the Cheddar.

Poached pears

Poach pears by peeling, removing the core and boiling in a large pan of water until soft. Add a little sugar and vanilla flavouring to the water if you want to serve the pears with a syrup. Remove pears from the pan, then keep simmering the syrup until reduced. Shortbread biscuits make a nice accompaniment.

Pear and blue cheese tarts

Perfect for lunch or a picnic, these little tarts are very easy to make.

- Using ready-made puff pastry, roll out four circles about 14 cm (5½ in) and score a border about 1 cm (⅓ in) in from the edge.
- Mash together 4 tbsp mascarpone and 50 g (2 oz) soft blue cheese then dot inside the border. Peel and slice 2 pears, then arrange on top on the pastry and cheese. Glaze with beaten egg.
- Bake in a preheated oven (200°C/400°F/gas mark 6) for 15 minutes, then scatter with a few pine nuts and a couple of sprigs of thyme. Cook for another 10–15 minutes until golden. Before serving, drizzle with a little honey.

Other ideas

- Add apples and pears to fruit jams and chutneys.
- Use pears in place of apples for pies, tarts and crumble desserts.
- Poach gently in either red wine or port and serve with port for a touch of luxury!
- Slice ripe pears in half and serve with hot custard or ice cream.
- Pear, Stilton, endive and walnut salad is a great winter treat. Drizzle with a little olive oil and an apple cider vinegar.

Soft fruits

Although we don't always consider soft fruits as part of the winter diet, with a little careful planning and baking, we can enjoy that touch of summer nearly all year round. Most soft fruits need a long and fairly sunny growing season to produce a good harvest, so a little tender loving care goes a long way especially if you live in a less than tropical climate.

Strawberries

Although traditionally a summer fruit, there are varieties of hybrid strawberries available from garden suppliers that will produce fruit from early summer right through to the early autumn. And any excess harvest can be made into the most wonderful jam to keep you going with summer fruit tastes throughout the winter months.

Strawberry plants are easy to grow and maintain and should provide you with bowls full of delicious strawberries just in time for the tennis season every year. Wild strawberries have been growing for thousands of years but wild plants don't produce sweet fruits. The sweeter varieties have been cultivated in the kitchen garden since around the 16th century. Don't be tempted to start off your strawberry bed with wild plants unless you are planning on making a lot of wild strawberry preserves, but even then, they will need a fair amount of extra sugar to make them sweet enough to eat.

Seed

It's rare to start strawberry beds from seed but it is possible. Buy seed from a reputable supplier and read the instructions on the packet before you start so you can give your plants the best possible conditions. Generally the seed should be sown in well-drained trays or pots of fresh compost and kept warm and watered until the plants are large enough to handle. They can then be transplanted into the garden or larger containers. Always wait until all danger of frost has passed before putting young plants outside.

Planting

There are many different varieties of strawberry available from heavy cropping smaller fruits to larger sweeter types. The smaller fruits are ideal if you have children to feed. There are some good strong hybrid plants available that keep cropping into late autumn.

Generally we tend to start a strawberry bed with plants bought from a nursery. Or, if you know someone who has been growing strawberries for a while, you may be able to save a few from their compost heap at the end of the growing season. Plants put out runners and a healthy strawberry bed needs thinning every year to keep producing healthy fruit.

Strawberries shouldn't be planted in soil that has grown peppers, potatoes or tomatoes during the previous few years. They share the same viruses and young plants can pick up a virus from the soil even before you get any fruit.

Find a sunny spot in the garden that you won't need for anything else during the next few years. A strawberry bed should be renewed every three years or so. The ground must be well drained and, if you have organic fertilizer or well-rotted manure, dig some into the soil a month or so before planting. Lightly dig over the soil just before planting. Strawberries are an ideal crop for raised beds. Plants tend to get straggly and are better contained if possible. Prepare the beds so you can reach the middle from both sides making them easier to maintain.

Put out your plants as soon as all danger of frost has passed and water well after planting. Allow at least 30 cm (12 in) between plants, and 45 cm (18 in) between rows. Double-check on growing recommendations for your particular variety. Make sure the roots are covered but the 'crown' of the plant is above the ground.

Care and maintenance

Keep weeds away and water your plants regularly in dry periods. When the plants have settled and are starting to grow, mulch around each one with dry straw. Don't pack it too closely; leave enough room for the plants to breathe and grow. The straw acts as a bed for your strawberry fruits and protects them from the damp of the soil and from slugs and snails.

ABOVE *This strawberry plant has ripe fruit ready for picking and many smaller fruits in the earlier stages of development.*

FAR LEFT *Strawberry plants can be planted in rows but are also happy in clumps or in pots and containers.*

When the fruits start growing they will need protection from birds as well. Net the whole bed with a wildlife-friendly netting, or if you haven't too many birds in your area, try hanging bird scarers, such as strings of old CDs and DVDs, over the bed to discourage them from stealing your fruit.

After the fruits have finished for the year, you can tidy up the bed by removing the runners. Runners are the baby plants sent out on long tendril-type stems from the mother plant. Cut these from the main plant with secateurs or a sharp pair of scissors and replant them. This should be done in the early autumn or after the plants have finished fruiting. These new plants can be left to find their own place to take root, but the bed will become untidy and possibly overcrowded, which tends to inhibit your crops from developing well in subsequent years.

A new bed should be established every few years, but by replanting the runners every year in a new bed, there will always be new young plants coming up. If older plants are still cropping well, leave them for a few more seasons, but when you notice they are producing less fruits, they should be removed, composted and the space used for something else.

Summer-cropping varieties of strawberries are vulnerable to the cold and the plants should be protected over the winter months with a cloche or other plastic covering. Remove the cloche in early spring and agitate the soil from time to time during the winter to avoid a build up of mould or stagnant water damaging your plants.

Harvesting

Many growers suggest that all fruits should be picked from your plants during the first year as soon as they appear. This is painful when you are just getting your plants going and looking forward to a few strawberries. But the plants will put more energy into developing the roots and crown and you will get better crops in subsequent years, so if you can bear it, pick those first fruits off before they ripen.

From the second year, pick your strawberries as soon as they are red all over. Protect from birds though, even at this late stage. After picking, recover with netting and adjust straw around the plants if necessary to stop fruits trailing on the soil.

Storing

Most soft fruits, including strawberries, are best eaten on the day they are picked but can be kept for a few days in a cool place if necessary. Later cropping varieties of strawberries will take the season right into late autumn with a little good weather, so won't need to be stored.

Strawberries can be frozen but lose a lot of texture during the process. Freeze quickly and store for a few months in the freezer. The most traditional way of storing soft fruits is in the form of preserves, jellies and jams. With a large heavy-based saucepan and a few sterilized jars in the kitchen, summer fruit jams can be made easily and stored for many months, if not years. Homemade preserves and jams also make great gifts, saving money and shopping stress.

Vitamins

Strawberries are packed with vitamins A and C and have long been used as a medicinal herb as well as a delicious sweet treat. They contain a natural anti-inflammatory, which has been shown to relieve symptoms in asthma and rheumatism sufferers. The leaves are used in tea infusions and the strawberry plant is also believed to relieve kidney disorders as well as throat infections. A small handful of strawberries will count as one of your five-a-day.

Recipe ideas

One of the best ways to store your garden strawberries is to make jam.

Strawberry Jam

To make jam you will need a heavy-based saucepan and sterilized jars, as well as a wooden spoon. A sugar thermometer is a handy tool to test the jam for the setting point but you can do without.

• Sterilize enough jars to hold about 2.25 kg (5 lb) jam before you start. Wash them well and rinse in hot water, then dry in a slow oven rather than using a tea towel or cloth.

• Remove leaves and stalks from 1.5 kg (3 lb) strawberries and rinse gently under running water. Cut into halves and drain, then put into a large heavy-based saucepan with the juice of half a lemon.

• Very carefully bring to the boil, stirring with a wooden spoon to prevent sticking. Reduce heat and simmer for about 25 minutes, or until the fruit is very soft. Stir every couple of minutes.

• Remove from the heat and stir in 1.5 kg (3 lb) sugar. Keep stirring until the sugar has dissolved. Return to the heat. Bring back to the boil and boil rapidly for about 20 minutes to reach setting point. If you have a sugar thermometer, this should read 105°C (221°F). If not, test for the setting point by dropping a small teaspoon of jam onto a cold saucer. After a few seconds, rub your thumb over the surface of the jam. If it wrinkles the jam has reached setting point; if not, boil rapidly for a few more minutes and test again.

• Pour or spoon the jam into warm jars. Don't put hot jam into cold jars as the glass may crack. Seal the lids and label.

• Store in a cool place out of direct light and use as soon as you want. A jar of strawberry jam makes an excellent gift at any time of year.

Other ideas

• Add a couple of strawberries to a smoothie. Bananas and strawberries go especially well together.

• Cut strawberries into halves or quarters and add to cereals, especially muesli.

• Turn a regular sponge cake into a glorious Victoria sponge. Cut strawberries into small pieces to mix with butter cream filling and decorate the top with a few strawberries cut in half.

• Garnish a green salad with a few strawberry halves.

• The best breakfast in the world must be a few hand-picked strawberries eaten while strolling round your garden early in the morning.

Blackberries

If you've ever had to deal with a bramble patch you may not feel very kindly towards blackberry bushes. There are, however, many hybrid varieties available that are thornless and will still produce juicy blackberries. Investigate different varieties at a good garden centre or through seed catalogues.

Blackberries have been collected from the wild for centuries and it's tempting to pick and eat them whenever we can. But with road pollution, chemical sprays on farmers' fields and other hazardous toxins floating about, blackberries really shouldn't be collected from anywhere other than a clean organic environment. In cooler climates, blackberries show up at the end of the summer and are usually ripening just in time to be cooked with the first windfalls from your apple trees.

Propagation

Blackberries can be tamed from the wild. If you are facing a bramble patch and want to salvage some plants, arm yourself with protective clothing and a sharp pair of shears before you start. Brambles seem to have a mind of their own and will happily trip you up or grab an exposed ankle with their long and very strong cable-like stems and seriously sharp thorns.

Seed

As all plants originally start from a seed of some kind, it is possible to start blackberry plants off with this method. However, it will be a long time before the plants will produce fruit and with many hybrid plants readily available, starting your crops from seed isn't the best method to use.

Layering

If you are hoping to propagate new plants from old, lay a branch along the ground and peg it down for a few months during the autumn and winter. In ideal conditions, by the following spring, the pegged branch should have produced roots. This can be cut from the mother plant and replanted if necessary, or left until the following autumn when it will be stronger and easier to transplant. If the surface of the soil is compact, dig a small hole to peg the branch into and cover with crumbly soil dug out of the hole.

Cuttings

As with most woody plants, blackberry plants can be started from cuttings. After the plants have finished fruiting in late autumn, cut 10–15 cm (4–6 in) stems from a healthy well-established plant. Push cuttings, cut end down, into well-drained pots of fresh compost. Keep watered but don't allow the pot to become waterlogged. Plant out during the following spring if the cuttings have developed roots. If the summer is promising to be a hot one though, keep the cuttings in pots and plant out during the following autumn. Keep watered and weed-free. Cuttings can be started in a seed bed but may need a little protection in winter.

The easiest way to start your blackberry crops is to buy plants from a reputable supplier. There are thornless varieties available and these really are better in a small garden, especially if you have young children.

Planting

Blackberries are one of the few plants that will produce a heavy crop of fruit even in very shady spots. They will, however, benefit from some sun and new

ABOVE *Brambles can develop their root systems from the stems and can grow in many different soil types except sandy soils.*

The usual planting time for blackberry canes is at the end of the summer or early autumn. Allow at least 45 cm (18 in) between plants, but double-check on any growing recommendations with your canes if you are buying them. Some giant varieties will need several metres of space. After planting, water well. Generally a well-established blackberry plant won't need much regular watering, however, newer hybrid varieties may need a little more attention. They shouldn't be allowed to dry out as they won't produce fruit.

Care and maintenance

Traditional blackberry plants trail and will crop more prolifically if they are supported. Train along a fence or wall or build a support system. Blackberries are useful to grow as barriers, especially the thorny varieties, or as dividing hedges in a larger garden. Blackberries have been part of the countryside's hedgerows for centuries, but because the hedgerows are disappearing fast, this is an ideal plant to rediscover and grow yourself.

Blackberries produce fruit on the second year branches. After fruits have been picked, the branches that produced the fruit should be cut down to the ground and the others left to produce fruit the following year.

Birds can be a problem with all fruit trees and shrubs. Protect your plants by netting with a wildlife-friendly net or use a bird scarer such as a string of shiny cd discs or silver foil, or get a cat.

Harvesting

Pick blackberries when they are purplish-black all over and come off the branches easily. When very ripe, the berries will drop into your hand at the slightest touch. Blackberries don't ripen after picking so only pick fully ripened fruits. Pick regularly so the plant develops

hybrid types won't be as hardy as wild plants. Check on positioning advice when you buy blackberry canes.

Soil isn't a problem either. The only soil blackberry plants don't really thrive well in is dry sandy soil. If your soil is dry and sandy, incorporate some well-rotted organic compost during the month or two before planting your canes. The ground should be fairly well drained but as blackberry plants flower late in the year, they are not affected by frost so won't mind a cold spot in the garden.

more fruit and older fruits don't rot on the branch. The first year's growth won't produce any fruit, but you may be able to buy a plant that has second-year branches. Plant in the autumn and you should get your first crop of blackberries the following summer.

Fruit is generally ready for picking from about mid-summer until late autumn depending on your region, climate conditions and the variety you are growing.

Storing

Blackberries will keep for a couple of days in the salad compartment of the fridge although they are better eaten on the day they are picked if possible. The berries can be frozen but a certain amount of texture and taste is lost during the process. Pick over the fruit, removing any leaves, stems and damaged fruit, then lay on freezer trays and freeze quickly. Once frozen, put into a container and label. They will keep in the freezer for several months until you want to make them into numerous delicious puddings and desserts.

Blackberries also make wonderful jam. Combine the berries with other fruits to produce your own special homemade preserves to give as gifts or store for a taste of summer through the winter months. Apples and blackberries are perfect fruits to combine in preserves or desserts.

ABOVE *Blackberries are a wonderful late summer to autumn treat, eaten as they are or made into many delicious desserts.*

Vitamins

Blackberries contain many vitamins and minerals and are particularly high in vitamin C. The fruits contain antioxidants that fight free radicals, helping to prevent certain cancers as well as heart disease, while the leaves have been used in alternative medicine for centuries. A cup of blackberry leaf tea every day will help boost the immune system and ward off colds and flu viruses, as well as alleviating minor digestive disorders.

Recipe ideas

Blackberries and apples are perfect together and, as they tend to be available at the same time of the year, it is well worth making the most of them.

Apple and Blackberry crumble
- To make a crumble mix, simply rub together 200 g (8 oz) plain flour and 100 g (4 oz) butter with your fingertips, then stir in 50 g (2 oz) sugar.
- Peel, core and slice apples and layer with prepared blackberries in an ovenproof dish. Cooking apples could be cooked for a few minutes beforehand if preferred. If the fruit is a little sharp-tasting, sprinkle over a spoonful or two of sugar along with a small amount of cinnamon if liked.
- Pile the crumble mix on top of the apples and blackberries and bake in a preheated medium oven 180°C (350°F/gas mark 4) for about 20–30 minutes. Try not to leave it in the oven too long as the crumble topping will burn.
- Serve hot or cold with cream, ice cream or warm custard. Use blackberries alone if there are no apples available and taste for sweetness before adding sugar.

Blackberry Alaska
This is a delicious yet simple recipe with wow-factor.
- Make or buy a plain 23 cm (9 in) sponge cake and put into an ovenproof dish that will double up as a serving dish.
- Spread vanilla ice cream over the top of the cake and level off. Cover and freeze until the ice cream is firm.
- While the ice cream is refreezing, beat together three egg whites until frothy, then slowly beat in 175 g (6 oz) sugar and keep beating until the mixture is stiff.
- Preheat the oven to 220°C (425°F/gas mark 7).
- Prepare the blackberries, removing any leaves or damaged fuit and place on top of the ice cream. Top with the meringue mix and spread to cover the ice cream and berries completely.

- Put into the preheated oven for 5 minutes until the meringue topping is slightly browned. Remove and serve immediately.

Blackberry pie
- Make a blackberry pie by piling prepared fruit in an ovenproof dish; sprinkle over 1–2 dessertspoons sugar.
- Cover with homemade or bought shortcrust pastry, using a pastry holder to keep the pastry off the fruit and therefore a little drier if preferred. Brush with beaten egg or milk to glaze.
- Bake in a preheated oven at 180°C (350°F/gas mark 4) for about 30 minutes or until golden brown.
- Sprinkle a little sugar over the pie soon after it comes out of the oven. Serve hot with custard or cold with cream or ice cream.

Other ideas
- If you make your own ice cream, add some blackberries to flavour it.
- Add a few blackberries to baked apples in the last ten minutes of cooking time. These are great at Halloween. The blackberry juice makes the apples look very gory!
- Use blackberry and apple when making a fruit loaf. Grate the apple and stir the blackberries carefully into the mixture after all other ingredients have been added.
- Mix crushed blackberries with butter cream when filling a sponge cake and use a few whole fruits to decorate the top.
- You can top all ice cream desserts or jellies with a few blackberries.
- Make blackberry jam to eat in the winter as a reminder of its wonderful late summer flavour.

Blackcurrants

Blackcurrants have been collected from wild plants for thousands of years. Since the Middle Ages, blackcurrants have been used in medicinal preparations and in the 19th and 20th centuries research has proved just how good this fruit is.

During World War Two, vitamin C was hard to come by in the UK and the government encouraged farmers and anyone who had some land to grow blackcurrants, since this berry is probably higher in vitamin C than any other fruit grown in cooler climates. Today, blackcurrants are one of the most widely grown commercial crops, providing children and adults with blackcurrant cordials and juices as well as being used in many alcoholic beverages and fruit desserts. They are an excellent crop to grow in a small garden as bushes take up relatively little space and will go on producing fruit for many years.

Propagation

Blackcurrants are generally started from canes from established plants. New hybrid varieties, available from good garden suppliers, produce currants the size of grapes and these larger fruits tend to contain more natural sugar so less added sugar is required when cooking with these berries.

Buy plants that grow well in your region. Check with your supplier and other growers in the area before you buy, if possible. If you do know local growers, they may be happy to donate some cuttings. Blackcurrant bushes need pruning once a year to keep them healthy, so you may be lucky to find healthy canes you can grow on to start your own blackcurrant bushes.

ABOVE *Taking cuttings from healthy blackcurrant plants is a common way of starting new plants.*

ABOVE *Blackcurrant canes like a sunny spot in the garden where the fruit will be exposed to full sun.*

RIGHT *Pick blackcurrants as soon as they turn black and use in many different dishes.*

Cuttings

Blackcurrant bushes are one of the most successful plants to propagate from cuttings. They are hardy and don't need protection during the winter, although if a very bad winter is expected it may be better to cover them with a cloche or other protection during the worst of the weather. Remove the cover as soon as the weather improves as they appreciate air flow and won't grow well if unventilated.

To start your blackcurrant patch using cuttings, you need to find a healthy bush. Don't use cuttings from a diseased or a weak plant. After all the fruits have been picked and leaves are falling off is the time to take cuttings – usually in mid-autumn in temperate climates, although leaving it a few weeks later is perhaps better. Fruit shrubs and trees are often planted in late autumn while the trees are at rest.

Choose a sunny spot in the garden. Blackcurrants will tolerate some shade but fruits won't develop quite as well. Avoid frost pockets and, although they like plenty of moisture, blackcurrants should never be allowed to become waterlogged. Prepare the ground by digging a trench about 15 cm (6 in) deep, add well-rotted organic matter if required. Soil should be slightly on the acid side for the best results. If you are buying hybrid plants, check on the manufacturer's growing recommendations before you start altering the acid/alkaline balance of your soil.

Cut 25 cm (10 in) stems from healthy branches with plenty of buds. The cuttings should be brown not green and the cut should be made just below a bud. Refer to the pruning advice under 'care and maintenance' (see page 138).

Plant a line of canes in your pre-dug trench allowing about 20–25 cm (8–10 in) between them. Ideally, each cane should have about four buds underground and two buds above the surface of the soil. Fill in the trench around the canes with the soil

that was dug out. Try not to damage the buds above or below the ground level. A little care at this point will ensure stronger, healthier plants. After planting, cut down the canes to leave just a couple of buds. This will seem drastic, but it helps to develop the root system.

Water well after planting and mulch around the canes to keep moisture in the ground. Don't mulch too close to the canes, since they need some air circulation. If you haven't any mulch available, old carpets or other similar material can be placed along the length of your row of canes on either side. Cuttings can be dug up in the following autumn and moved to another position if required. Bought plants should be planted in a similar way as cuttings, but again check on any manufacturer's growing advice for variations.

Care and maintenance

Blackcurrants love water and should never be allowed to dry out, especially in the summer months when they are producing fruit. Use mulch if you have some to keep moisture in the ground and always remove weeds as they will be drawing water from the soil and taking it from your plants.

Leave the plants to grow for the first year and then in subsequent years they should be pruned to keep them healthy and producing plenty of fruit. Generally your plants need about 20 percent of the wood cut out from the middle of the plant and a little more from the outside. Use sharp secateurs and remove any damaged or unhealthy-looking branches, as well as those that cross in the middle. Keep air circulation in mind when pruning blackcurrants.

As long as your plants get plenty of water, air circulation and are pruned carefully once a year, they should provide plenty of luscious blackcurrants for many years to come.

Harvesting

Pick blackcurrants as soon as they are black. Collect on a sunny day as wet blackcurrants rot very quickly. Blackcurrant leaves, for blackcurrant leaf tea, can be picked through the year. Young leaves are preferable but never take too many leaves from one plant at one time otherwise the plant will put more energy into producing foliage than fruits.

Storing

To store blackcurrants for a few days, pick a whole truss of fruits and put in the salad compartment of the fridge. They will keep for 4 or 5 days, although they are best eaten as soon as possible after picking.

Leaves can be dried by hanging in a dry airy place and then crumbling into a labelled jar. Blackcurrant fruits can also be successfully stored in the form of pies, jams or even wines.

Vitamins

These unassuming little currants are packed with vitamin C, having one of the highest levels of all fruits, while also being less acidic than citrus fruits. They have significant quantities of calcium and iron, are rich in antioxidants and are generally a healthy crop to grow. Because of their high vitamin content, use the currants in cordials and other recipes to bottle or freeze for the winter months.

Blackcurrant leaf tea is popular and can alleviate some minor digestive complaints. Put a few chopped fresh or dried leaves in a jug and pour over boiling water. Cover and leave to infuse for 5 minutes. Strain into a cup. A spoonful of honey can be added if liked.

Recipe ideas

One of the most well-known commercial uses for blackcurrants is blackcurrant juice. However, if you grow your own blackcurrants there's no reason why you shouldn't try making it yourself.

Blackcurrant ice lollies

Kids will love these lollies. Homemade with blackcurrants from your own garden and packed with vitamin C, you won't need to worry about nasty additives that sometimes come with this sort of food.

- Remove all stems and damaged fruits and put blackcurrants in a pan. Add sugar if you are growing a variety that isn't sweet enough on its own. Allow about 200 g (8 oz) sugar to 450 g (1 lb) blackcurrants.
- Cover with water and cook over a low heat until the sugar is dissolved. Bring almost to the boil, reduce heat and simmer gently for 5 minutes until the fruit is soft.
- Add the grated rind and juice of a lemon and continue to simmer for another 5 minutes.
- Leave it to cool for 10 minutes then strain into a warm sterilized bottle. Seal and leave to cool completely. Pour homemade blackcurrant juice into lolly moulds or ice cube trays with a lolly stick in each compartment. Freeze and use as required.

Blackcurrant purée

This simple purée can be used to mix with other desserts such as homemade ice cream or take the place of jam in 'jam' tarts.

- Prepare 200 g (8 oz) blackcurrants and cook gently with a couple of tablespoons of water until soft. Push through a sieve or blend in a food processor. This will make about 150 ml (5 fl oz) purée.
- To make a special creamy dessert, add the juice of half an orange when cooking blackcurrants. Then when the purée is cool, stir in 75 g (3 oz) icing sugar and 300 ml (10 fl oz) whipped cream. Put the mixture into a freezer container and freeze until firm.

Other ideas

- Remember to use leaves for a beneficial herbal tea.
- Use blackcurrants in pies mixed with other fruits or on their own.
- Blackcurrants are especially good for open tarts and flans. Make large family tarts or individual jam-type tartlets. Cook blackcurrants first in water and sugar if needed and mash gently. Fill pastry cases and cook until pastry is golden brown.
- Add power-packed vitamins to the start of your day by mixing a handful of blackcurrants to your breakfast smoothie.
- Blend blackcurrants with a little honey in a food processor and use to top ice cream or other desserts.
- Stir blackcurrants into a fruit salad.
- Blackcurrants also make wonderful jam. Follow the strawberry jam recipe on page 129 or use an old family favourite. Home-grown blackcurrants made into homemade jam must be the best possible winter preserve you can have in the cupboard during the cold months of the year.

Resources and further reading

More books by the author

Grow Your Own Groceries
published by Spring Hill Books
Grow Your Own Pharmacy
published by Findhorn Press
Herb Gardening
published by Crowood Press
Granny's Book of Good Old Fashioned Common Sense
published by Black & White Publishing

Further reading

The Practical Garden Encyclopaedia
published by Colour Library

Complete Garden Manual
published by Collins

Useful websites
www.flower-and-garden-tips.com
www.botanical.com
www.bbc.co.uk/gardening
www.gardenaction.co.uk
www.nutrition.org.uk
www.nutrition.gov
www.5aday.nhs.uk

Index

Acknowledgements – picture credits

Front cover image: Alamy
Back cover images: Turnip – Garden Picture Library;
Carrots and Brussels Sprout – Alamy
Title page: Alamy
Page 7: Garden Picture Library
Page 8: Garden Picture Library
Page 11: Garden Picture Library
Page 12: Alamy
Page 15: Alamy
Page 16: iStockphoto
Page 21: Alamy
Page 24: Alamy
Page 25: iStockphoto
Page 27: Alamy
Page 30: Alamy
Page 33: Garden Picture Library
Pages 34–36: Alamy
Pages 39–41: Alamy
Page 43: Garden Picture Library
Pages 45–47: Garden Picture Library
Pages 51–52: Garden Picture Library
Page 56: Garden Picture Library
Page 57: Alamy
Page 58: Garden Picture Library
Page 60: Alamy

Pages 63–65: Garden Picture Library
Page 69: Alamy
Page 70: Garden Picture Library
Page 71: Alamy
Page 72: Garden Picture Library
Page 74: Alamy
Pages 77–78: Garden Picture Library
Pages 82–84: Alamy
Page 87: Alamy
Page 89: Garden Picture Library
Pages 90–94: Alamy
Pages 97–98: Alamy
Pages 101–103: Garden Picture Library
Page 105: iStockphoto
Pages 107–109: Garden Picture Library
Page 111: Alamy
Page 113: Garden Picture Library
Pages 114–116: Alamy
Page 119: (top) iStockphoto; (bottom) Garden Picture Library
Page 121: Alamy
Pages 122–127: Garden Picture Library
Page 129: iStockphoto
Pages 131–132: Garden Picture Library
Page 133: Alamy